The 50 Keys to Learning SAS® Stored Processes

First Edition

Tricia Aanderud
Angela Hall

The 50 Keys to Learning SAS® Stored Processes, First Edition

ISBN-10: 0615588727   ISBN-13: 9780615588728

First Printing: April 2012

Produced in the United States of America.

Trademarks

SAS is a registered trademark of SAS Institute, Inc.

All terms mentioned in this book that are known to be trademarks or service marks have been appropriately capitalized. The publisher or authors cannot attest to the accuracy of this information. Use of a term in this book should not be regarded as affecting the validity of any trademark or service mark.

Warning and Disclaimer

Every effort has been made to make this book as complete and as accurate as possible, but no warranty or fitness is implied. The information provided is on an "as is" basis. The authors and the publisher shall have neither liability nor responsibility to any person or entity with respect to any loss or damages arising from the information contained in this book or programs accompanying it.

Authors

Tricia Aanderud
Angela Hall

Editor

Rene' Cherny

Technical Reviewers

Don Henderson, Henderson Consulting Services, LLC
Karen Hinkson, SAS Institute, Inc.
Stephen Overton, Zencos Consulting, LLC
Juli Yaguda, Zencos Consulting, LLC

Dedication

To the SAS community, full of helpful, inventive, and challenging minds, who provide an endless source of inspiration.

Acknowledgements

We would like to acknowledge the help and support of our excellent technical reviewers, Don, Steve, Karen, and Juli; also our dedicated and tireless technical editor, Rene'.

Other Publications by These Authors

Books

- Building Business Intelligence with SAS: Content Development Examples, SAS Press

Blogs

- Angela's Real BI for Real Users, *http://blogs.sas.com/content/bi/*

- Tricia's Business Intelligence Notes for SAS BI Users, *http://www.bi-notes.com*

Additional Resources

- SAS Support Site, *http://support.sas.com*

- SAS Community, *http://www.sascommunity.org*

Accessing the Code Samples in the Book

After you register your book, you can download the code samples used in this book.

Use these instructions:

1. Navigate to this page using a Web browser:

   http://www.bi-notes.com/stp-book-email-list

2. When prompted, enter the following password:

   50-Keys-STP-Book

3. Use your email address to register the book.

4. When you have confirmed your email address, you will receive a link and a password to download the ZIP file.

Contents

Introduction

From the first day we discussed writing this book, we have been excited because we are very enthusiastic about stored processes. They are fun to write because they are so flexible and add a completely new dimension to your SAS programs. In this book, we show you how easy it is to convert simple reports into a complex, flexible, and interactive SAS stored process that will impress your end users.

As you read this book, you will find keys that will increase your understanding of what is important about the stored process technique. You will also find additional tips you can implement later.

SAS Institute Inc. packages the stored process technology within the SAS Integration Technologies and includes it automatically within many SAS solutions, including Business Intelligence (BI) and Customer Intelligence (CI). This technology makes it easy to create flexible and interactive reports to use with the SAS (BI) clients, a Web browser, and much more.

Who Should Use This Book

If you are a beginner or have already created basic stored processes, this book guides you through simple and advanced techniques for creating stored processes. We introduce a foundation example, and many of the subsequent examples build on that example. This helps you understand how to evolve a simple stored process into a complex stored process. This book provides ideas for integrating stored process with the various SAS BI clients and guides you through some common troubleshooting techniques.

We assume that you have some familiarity with writing programs using the SAS language and using the SAS macro language in programs. You do not need prior experience creating SAS Stored Processes or with the SAS Prompt Framework to understand the examples. Our examples provide guidance and clarity so that you can quickly convert your own SAS programs into SAS stored processes.

In later chapters, we share ways to use stored processes with Web forms, and you will need some familiarity with HTML and JavaScript. If you are not familiar with either language, you can use a Web search engine, such as Google, to find examples, tutorials, and other reference information.

Although we are not JavaScript experts, we have located code snippets on the Web with enough documentation to complete our stored process. Using the examples in this book, you can easily change the sample code to work with your code.

How this Book is Organized

This book helps you navigate through SAS code conversion to creating a SAS stored process to generating custom Web applications. The chapters are arranged in logical groups to help you progress from simple to complex concepts.

Chapters	Summary
1 – 3	Explains stored process development basics.
4 – 5	Shows how to improve stored process appearance and perform troubleshooting.
6 – 9	Explains how to run stored processes from the SAS BI clients.
10 - 12	Describes how to improve interactions within the stored process. In addition, specific use cases for making custom outputs and useful reporting applications are included.

Using the Examples in this Book

All example code is shown in a table so that the left column contains the actual code and the right column explains what the code is doing or how the code was updated to make it work with the stored process. Gray shaded areas indicate that the code remains the same, and white areas show how the code was updated to make it even more powerful.

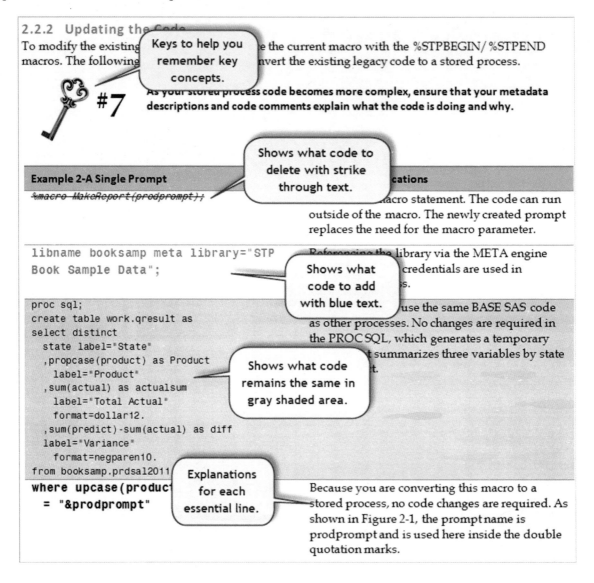

Prerequisites

To re-create the examples in this book, you must have access to the following:

- SAS Management Console 9.3 or SAS Enterprise Guide 5.1 in order to register your stored process.

- Code storage location on the SAS Server. This is a physical folder on the server where you have *Write* access to save your stored process code. See Section 1.3.2, "Using the Source Code Repository" for additional details.

- Data tables defined in a metadata library. See Section 1.3.3, "Accessing Data Libraries" for additional details.

Setting up the Book Examples

You can access the example code in this book from the companion Website (http://www.bi-notes.com) in a ZIP file. All of the SAS program names in this file are comprised of the chapter numbers, the order within the chapter, and a short title. For example, if the chapter refers to "Example 2-A Single Prompt", you will find a SAS program called "2_a_Single_Prompt" in the ZIP file.

When using the examples in the book, you might want to create a new stored process for each example, or you can keep building upon the previous example.

Our examples are based on the sample data tables that are shipped with SAS BI clients. We registered a sample data library called BOOKSAMP in the SAS Management Console, and the following data tables (with the noted changes) are included:

- PRDSALE2011

  This is a copy of the SASHELP.PRDSAL3 data table with the date values changed from 1997-1998 to 2010-2011. Use the following code to create this data table for use with the samples:

  ```
  libname booksamp 'C:\SAS\Data\STPSamples';
  data booksamp.prdsal2011;
  set sashelp.prdsal3;
  Year=Year+13;
  Date=intnx('Month', date, 156);
  run;
  ```

- STOCKS

  This dataset is available from the SASHELP library. No modifications were made to the data.

- CANDY_SALES_SUMMARY

  This data table is located in *<SAS Enterprise Guide installation directory>*\SAMPLES\DATA. In order to complete several of the examples, we duplicated this data and modified the dates. Included below is the sample code to create 2011.

  ```
  libname booksamp 'C:\SAS\Data\STPSamples';
  libname candy 'C:\Program Files\SAS\EnterpriseGuide\4.3\Sample\Data';
  data booksamp.salesdetail2011(drop=day);
  set candy.candy_sales_summary;
  Fiscal_Year='2011';
  day=day(date);
  Date=mdy(Fiscal_Month_Num, day, Fiscal_Year);
  run;
  ```

Using SAS Version 9.3

In SAS 9.3, SAS Institute introduced new functionality for stored processes. To use these features, you must create the stored processes using the SAS Management Console 9.3 or SAS Enterprise Guide 5.1.

All of the programs in this book run in SAS 9.3 ; however, much of the functionality is available in prior versions. Stored process developers using SAS 9.2 and prior versions can use this book to understand stored process development and methodology.

The following table compares SAS 9.3 stored process functionality to SAS 9.2 and prior versions.

9.3 Functionality	9.2 and Prior Versions Functionality
The application automatically determines the server and output type.	Users chose the server and output when registering the stored process.
SAS Workspace Server has streaming output capabilities.	Users assign Web-based output to the SAS Stored Process Server specifically.
SAS stored process code no longer needs the *ProcessBody; comment.	Users must add the *ProcessBody; comment to the code when assigning a stored process to the SAS Workspace Server.
Stored Process Reports containing cached stored process output are available.	All streaming stored process output is refreshed at each run request, while all permanent packages are stored for use.
The STP procedure allows you to call a stored process from other SAS code, such as during the batch process.	Users cannot run a stored process from a batch process or call another stored process.
The DATA value for the _action macro variable was added to return metadata about the stored process.	Information is available in metadata; however, it requires programming to retrieve.

If you are operating in a SAS 9.3 environment with SAS Enterprise Guide 4.3 or SAS Add-in to Microsoft Office 4.3, the stored process must be made compatible with SAS 9.2 version. You must register the stored process from SAS Enterprise Guide 4.3 or convert a stored process from the SAS Management Console. See Section 5.6.1, "Making 9.3 Stored Processes Compatible for 4.3 Clients" for details about how to convert a stored process.

Differences in Stored Processes Wizards

In Chapter 1, "Getting Started with Stored Processes", this book shows how to use the wizard for SAS Management Console 9.3. The wizard menus in Enterprise Guide 5.1 and SAS Management Console 9.3 are identical.

In Chapter 6, "Using SAS Enterprise Guide" the book demonstrates how to use Enterprise Guide 4.3. The wizard menus in Enterprise Guide 4.3 and SAS Management Console 9.2 are identical.

Chapter

1

Getting Started with
Stored Processes

SAS Stored Processes are SAS programs stored in a central location and shared by multiple clients. You can access a stored process from SAS BI clients, from Web applications, from SAS Enterprise Guide, and other locations. When you run a stored process from any of these locations, you ensure a consistent data table or report. Because the applications that access the data are stored in a central, secure location, the organization knows that their data is safe.

Additionally, when the SAS program is stored in a central location, changes to the stored process code flows through the entire system. This helps organizations consolidate programming silos into one location, which reduces duplication and increases efficiency.

In this chapter, you will learn how to access and run a stored process. Then, we walk you through steps to register a stored process in the SAS Management Console. As you use the examples in this book, consult this chapter as you create and edit stored processes.

1.1 Accessing and Running a Stored Process

Users can access and run stored processes from multiple locations. In some cases, the stored process might be transparent to the user.

There are multiple ways to use stored processes, including the following:

- **SAS Enterprise Guide**

    From within SAS Enterprise Guide, you can create, edit or run a stored process. In Chapter 6, "Using SAS Enterprise Guide" you will learn different ways to use SAS Enterprise Guide to work with stored processes.

- **SAS BI Clients**

    You can leverage SAS Stored Processes for reports, output, or data with SAS Information Map Studio, SAS Web Report Studio, SAS Information Delivery Portal, SAS Add-in for Microsoft Office, and SAS Business Intelligence Dashboard. In Chapter 7, "Using SAS BI Clients" and Chapter 8, "Using the SAS BI Web Clients" you will see multiple examples of stored process use in the BI clients.

- **SAS Stored Process Web Application**

  You can use a Web browser to access stored processes from the SAS Stored Process Web Application. See Section 1.1.1, "Accessing a Stored Process from the Web" to see an example.

- **Other methods**

  There are other methods to access SAS Stored Processes. Using Web services, such as SAS BI Web Services using XMLA or structured Web services, you can call stored processes. In addition, you can use the SAS Stored Process Java API or SAS Stored Process Windows API to develop custom applications to access and run SAS Stored Processes.

  These advanced topics are beyond the scope of this book; however, you can check the SAS Support Site for more information. Don Henderson has written advanced information about SAS Stored Processes, which are available from SAS Publishing.

1.1.1 Accessing a Stored Process from the Web

The SAS Stored Processes are available from the SAS Stored Process Web Application Website that lists the registered stored processes. Use a Web browser to navigate to the SAS Stored Process Web Application home page. This page is in a location similar to the following:

> `http://MachineName:PortNumber/SASStoredProcess/do`

The following figure shows the default Welcome window, which lists the SAS Stored Process samples and the available stored processes.

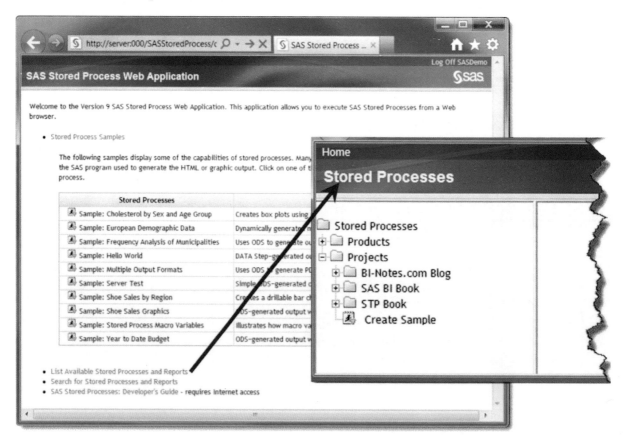

Figure 1-1 Accessing stored processes

Your organization might have changed these pages as they can be customized. If no changes have been made, try some of the samples in the list. Otherwise, contact your SAS administrator for help locating the SAS sample stored processes.

 #1 | **To skip the Welcome window, bookmark the following URL to go the Stored Processes Webpage directory structure:** http://*MachineName:PortNumber*/SASStoredProcess/do?_action=index

To access the stored processes registered by your organization, select **List Available Stored Processes and Reports**. In the Stored Processes page, use the navigation menu to access the stored processes. In this example, you can see that the Stored Process folder contains several sub-folders to assist with organization. A single stored process called Created Sample resides at the bottom of the folder structure. You will learn other ways to use the SAS Stored Process Web Application in Section 5.1, "Using the SAS Stored Process Web Application".

1.1.2 Using the Search Functionality

Use the SAS Stored Processes Welcome window (see Figure 1-1) to access the list of stored process and the search functionality. Select **Search for Stored Processes and Reports** on the Welcome window to access the Stored Process Search window (Figure 1-2), where you can search for a specific stored process based on various criteria. The search only returns the stored processes you have permission to access.

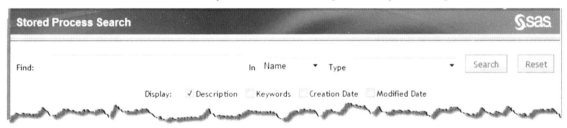

Figure 1-2 Using the search page

1.1.3 Running a Stored Process

Use a Web browser to navigate to the location of a stored process and select its name. In this example, the stored process name is *Create Sample*. This stored process does not have any associated prompts, so the output appears immediately, as shown in Figure 1-3. In later chapters, you will learn alternate ways to run a stored process.

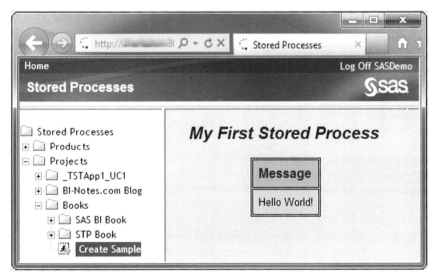

Figure 1-3 Running the Create Sample stored process

When you run a stored process, several things happen behind the scenes (shown in Figure 1-4). Let's consider the Create Sample stored process. After logging into the SAS Logon Manager, the SAS Metadata Server verifies your access level and the SAS Stored Process Web Application appears. When you run Create Sample from the SAS Stored Process Web Application, the metadata available on the SAS Metadata Server provides the stored process code physical location and ensures that you have proper access to the location data tables and that the libraries exists. The SAS Stored Process Application Server runs the stored process code using needed data and returns the results to the SAS Stored Process Web Application.

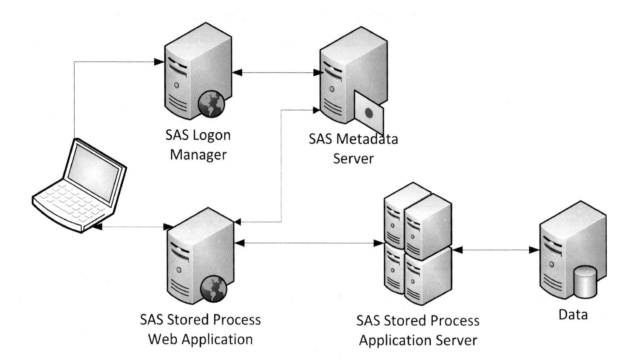

Figure 1-4 SAS Service interactions

1.2 Registering a Stored Process

When you register a stored process, you provide information to the SAS Metadata Server about the stored process name, stored process code physical location, prompts associated with the stored process, and so on. This information is called metadata. The server then executes a stored process using this information.

You can use SAS Management Console or SAS Enterprise Guide to register your stored process. The prompts and process are essentially the same. SAS code is written, information about the stored process is registered within the metadata, and any needed prompts are created.

Within SAS 9.3, the code can be stored within the metadata directly or as a separate .sas file on the physical server. It has been noted that during development it is more efficient to use a separate .sas file, as changes are immediately available without refreshing your metadata connection by logging out and logging back into the environment.

1.2.1 Using SAS Management Console

Use the New Stored Process wizard to register the stored process by following these steps:

1. Select Actions > New > Stored Process to open the **Create New SAS Stored Process Wizard** window.

    Note: You can also right-click on the target metadata folder where you would like to save the stored process and choose New > Stored Process as shown in the following figure.

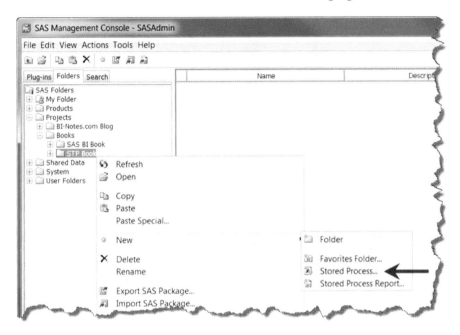

2. In the New SAS Stored Process window, type the stored process name and describe the stored process. Select **Next** to continue.

The name used appears in the list. Choose a name that explains what the stored process does so that users can locate it quickly. The remaining fields are optional.

Notes:

*   It is a good practice to provide keywords that help users locate the stored process and to note who is responsible for it.

*   You can add spaces to your stored process name, but some Web browsers might not honor the space and truncate the stored process name, which can cause the stored process to fail.

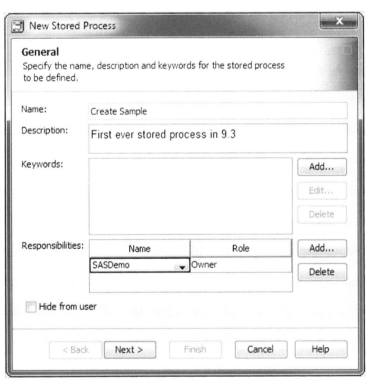

3. Select the server that the stored process uses, where the SAS program resides, and the stored process output from the Execution window shown in the following window.

   Note: The numbers in the figure correspond to the table numbers following the figure.

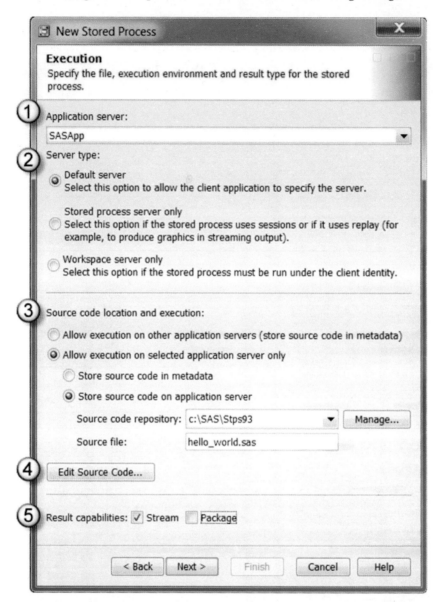

	Field	Description
1	Application server	Select the server that executes the stored process, typically SASApp. Some organizations might have defined multiple application servers. Consult your SAS administrator for further guidance.
2	Server type	Select a server to host the stored process or allow the application to make the selection.
		Default server Starting with SAS 9.3, you can allow the client application to determine the server.
		Stored Process Server This server uses streaming output to push results

Field	Description
	directly to the Webpage or other clients. It completes requests under one user identity, SASSRV. There are certain features that are only supporting using the stored process server. When examples within this book require this selection, we will explicitly state to choose Stored Process Server.
	Workplace Server A single-user server where each request initiates a new server process. All users are subject to host operating system permissions, which provides increased security.
	See Section 1.2.3, "Understanding Server Types" for more information about the capabilities and advantages of each server type.
3 Source code location and execution	Select where the stored process code is stored and runs.
	Allow execution on other applications servers Select to allow the stored process to run on multiple application servers. You must store the source code in the metadata when you select this choice. Select the **Edit Source Code** button to enter your SAS code.
	Allow execution on selected application server only Select to control which application server runs the stored process. There are two options:
	• **Store source code in metadata**
	Save the source code in the metadata. Select **Edit Source Code** to enter your SAS code.
	• **Store source code on application server**
	Save the .sas program in a source code repository. Specify the source code repository and type the program name in the Source File field.
	You must have *Write* access to the source code repository folder where your code is stored. See Section 1.3.2, "Using the Source Code Repository" for more details about source code repositories.
4 Edit source code	Select **Edit Source Code** to open a window where you can type or paste your stored process code. See Section 1.2.4, "Using the Source Code" for an example of the Source Code Editor window.
5 Result capabilities	Select the result based on the output that the stored process generates. You can select one either or both types.
	See Section 1.2.5, "Understanding the Result Capabilities" for additional information on the stored process results.

4. You can use the Parameters window to create, delete, and edit the prompts. Select Parameters from the New Stored Process window.

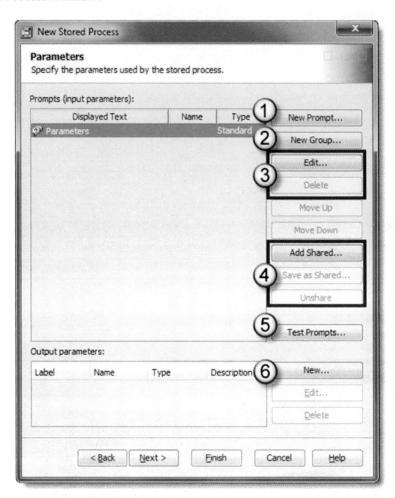

	Field	Description
1	New Prompt	Use to create a prompt. You can create a variety of prompts, such as text, date, or numeric. In Chapter 2, "Creating Simple Stored Processes", you will learn how to use a text and date range prompt in a stored process.
2	New Group	Use to create grouped prompts. In Chapter 3, "Making Decisions with Code", you will learn how to use a grouped prompt in a stored process.
3	Edit Prompts	Use to work with existing prompts. After creating a prompt, use these buttons to modify or delete the prompt. In Section 4.2.1, "Removing Grouped Prompts", you will see an example of this functionality.
4	Add Shared Prompts	Use to work with shared prompts. In Chapter 4, "Controlling Output and Graphic Options", you will learn about shared prompts.
5	Test Prompts	Use to see how the prompts appear and to confirm if displays as expected.
6	Output parameters	Use to work with output parameters. In Section 7.1.2, "Adding Prompts to an Information Map", you will learn how to use this option with an information map.

5. Select **Next** to display the Data window. In this window, you can specify additional data sources or data for targets that you can define.

    In some cases, the SAS Stored Process needs to work with other data sources, such as a range of cells within Microsoft Excel, or make data available to subsequent process, such as forwarding data to another SAS stored process. In Section 7.3, "Using the SAS Add-In for Microsoft Office" you will learn more about how to use this functionality with a Microsoft Excel spreadsheet.

    Using these additional data source options from the stored process code and prompts can offer significant value and usability.

6. Select **Finish** to register the stored process.

    In Section 1.1.1, "Accessing a Stored Process from the Web", you can see an example of this stored process with the output.

1.2.2 Using SAS Enterprise Guide
If you are using Enterprise Guide 4.3, see Chapter 6, "Using SAS Enterprise Guide" for more details about registering a stored process.

Note: See the Introduction for additional notes about the compatibility differences between the Stored Process Wizard.

1.2.3 Understanding Server Types
Two servers are available to run a stored process: Stored Process Server and Workplace Server. Each server has some different capabilities that might work better for your specific situation.

Using the Stored Process Server

The Stored Process Server is a multi-user server using a single shared identity for all requests. It uses streaming output, which pushes the results directly to a Web page or to other clients. This server supports sessions and streaming graphic output. You will learn more about data access and called sessions, in Section 9.3, "Using Sessions".

A single identity (in default installations this is SASSRV) is used to initiate all stored processes and this account will need access to underlying physical data. It is common for administrators to view this server as less secure however, the end user must still have proper metadata access to view and execute the stored process. For data sources, it is a best practice that all references to data libraries are not pre-defined but are specified in the stored process code as META librefs. More information about using the META LIBREF is available in Section 1.3.3, "Accessing Data Libraries".

Using the Workspace Server

The Workspace Server completes each stored process as a single-user in a separate server process. This method offers higher security because it uses the credentials specific to the user. You might want additional security when the stored process accesses sensitive data, such as employee salaries.

Starting with SAS 9.3, the Workspace Server can stream output and Web services. From this server, you can execute client-submitted SAS code and access data. In addition, you can use this server with information maps. See Section 7.1, "Working with the SAS Information Map Studio", for more information.

1.2.4 Using the Source Code Window

Use the Source Code window to add or modify the source code. In the Execution tab, after you indicate the method you want to use, select Edit Source Code to access the Source Code Window. Use this simple text editor to type the code or copy and paste it from another location. If you need to change this code, select Edit Source Code to make any necessary changes. In addition, you can edit the stored process code directly in the logical location using a text editor, such as Notepad. You can also use SAS Enterprise Guide or BASE SAS to edit stored process code.

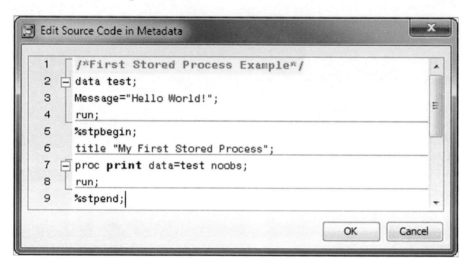

Figure 1-5 Source Code in Metadata window

1.2.5 Understanding the Result Capabilities

The stored process engine can write output to two different locations. You can select one or both options depending on how your stored process is used.

Stream   Use this result to write the output via a data stream to the client, such as an HTML or XML file, which is immediately available to view in a Web page.

Package   Use this result to write the output to a package that users can view. A package can be any combination of datasets, images, and files. Both servers can use this method.

There are two package types and different reserved macros are used to define which type is produced by the stored process.

- **Transient output** is available when the client connects to the server. This is a good way to deliver text and graphic output. After it is no longer in use, the system removes the content.

- **Permanent output** is stored in a location, such as WebDAV repository or a server file system. This output is available any time and can be published to a channel or sent as email. You can add security to the file, such as assigning a user name and password. Starting in SAS 9.2, you can use a prompt to supply the necessary information for creating a permanent package. See Section 9.1, "Using Background Processing" for more details.

1.3 Understanding the Stored Process Support Structure

Underlying the stored process system is an architecture that includes SAS metadata. All metadata is stored within the SAS Metadata Server. Using the SAS Management Console, SAS Administrators use the SAS Management Console to control how the stored process developers access source code and data tables.

You must have *WriteMetadata* access to the metadata location; otherwise, you will not be able to register the stored process. From the SAS Management Console, a SAS administrator can create source code repositories and assign permissions.

#2 Before creating a stored process, ensure that you have *WriteMetadata* access to the SAS folder in which the stored process will be stored.

1.3.1 Understanding Metadata

In the SAS Management Console, SAS administrators define and maintain the metadata and folder structure. Metadata is essentially data about data, and it can be many things. The following are examples of metadata:

- User access and security information

- Structure information with reference to how everything runs and is organized

- Pointers to physical files or data table locations

  Libraries are data folders that represent one or more specific folders on the server. The physical path could be *c:\SAS\data\my project* or *//srvdata1/projects/stp book*. However, the user only sees the path defined for the metadata but not the actual physical path.

It is important to understand that the proper access to metadata libraries must be granted (such as *Read* and *ReadMetadata* access) for the end user to receive results.

1.3.2 Using the Source Code Repository

From the Execution window, you can specify which source code repository you want to store the SAS file associated with your stored process. A source code repository is the physical location of the SAS file and there may be more than one. In Figure 1-6 you can see the hello_world.sas program in the source code repository.

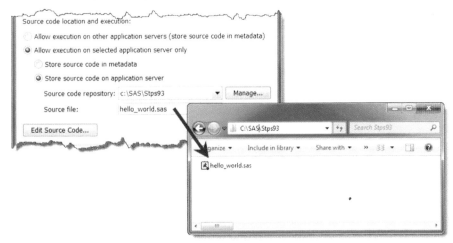

Figure 1-6 Source code repository

1.3.3 Accessing Data Libraries

Stored processes can use base libraries or metadata libraries to access the data tables. In order for stored processes to access data, a SAS administrator must assign and allow permission to the data library. When a library is pre-assigned, a single user ID (SASSRV) assigns the LIBREF. When the SAS Object Spawner service starts, it pre-assigns all libraries, which is similar to the AUTOEXEC.SAS file used in BASE SAS. In most environments, this is not a good idea because you may grant permission to libraries that you do not want all users to see. Refer to the SAS Support Site for more information about metadata libraries.

 #3 When a RDBMS library is pre-assigned, a shared identity is used to establish the connection. If users need to authenticate individually then leverage the META library type.

A preferred option is to define the LIBREFs using the META library type, so that the user running the stored process is verified having *Read* and *ReadMetadata* access to the library at run time.

Using code similar to that shown below, modifying the *LIBREF* value with an appropriate name and replacing the @name area to match the exact library name defined in your server list.

```
libname libref meta library="@name" metaout=data;
```

For example, to indicate the STP Book Sample Data metadata library, add the following to your stored process code. This code calls the metadata library shown in Figure 1-7.

```
libname booksamp meta library='STP Book Sample Data' metaout=data;
```

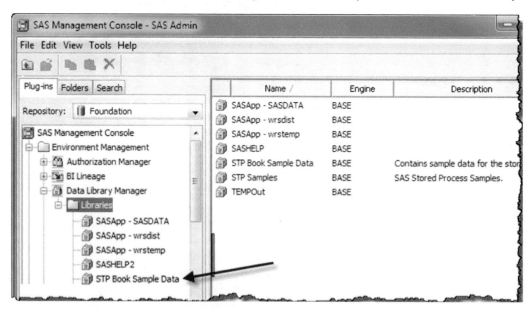

Figure 1-7 SAS Management Console Metadata Library

 #4 When using metadata libraries, assign each LIBREF within the stored process code using the LIBNAME meta technique.

In Section 5.6, "Accessing Data in Libraries", you will learn about the errors that occur when user access is not available.

Creating Simple Stored Processes

BASE SAS gives programmers the exponential ability to query and report about data from their desktops; however, this limitation means that a user can access the data from their desktops only. As an organization's reporting needs grow, more individuals need to quickly retrieve and analyze similar information. As a result, a small group with access to the data unintentionally becomes *report gatekeepers*. Other members of the organization have to talk to these gatekeepers for even the simplest piece of data.

Before you convert a SAS program to a stored process, you must consider whether the program is a good candidate for conversion. Although any SAS program can be a stored process, this does not mean that all programs should be a stored process. Programs that require user input, run on user demand, and generate output are typically better candidates than those programs scheduled to run overnight, take a long time to run or require no user modifications.

In Chapter 1, "Getting Started with Stored Processes" you learned how to register a stored process. In this chapter, you will convert an existing SAS program into a stored process and apply different prompt types to increase the scope and flexibility of a program.

2.1 Sample Scenario for Stored Process Conversion

As an example of a report gatekeeper and how a stored process solved the issue, let's consider the following business scenario. There is a SAS program that exports returned hardware parts from an enterprise database to a spreadsheet. Each time a reliability analyst reviews a part with a high return rate, a SAS programmer adds the part number to the where statement, reruns the program, and sends the spreadsheet to the analyst. The analyst retrieves the data and begins the analysis process.

After the program was converted to a stored process, the reliability analyst could access the stored process using the web interface or even the SAS Add-In for Microsoft Office application. Within moments of selecting the desired product from a drop-down list, the analyst is able to start reviewing the results; thus, adding automation to the business process. In addition, the stored process allows the analyst to access the report faster, and the SAS programmer can continue to work on other tasks; thus, increasing the business efficiency.

 #5 **SAS programs that require user input, run on demand, or require up to date output immediately are all great candidates for converting to stored processes**

The program in this scenario was an excellent candidate for converting into a stored process. By using a single prompt, the stored process essentially asked the reliability analyst which product to retrieve.

Because the stored process prompts the user, other reliability analysts can also use this same report, except they would have data specific to their specific needs.

2.2 Creating a Stored Process with a Single Prompt

In the first example, you duplicate the previous business scenario by converting an existing program that uses a single prompt into a stored process for your new customer: a large North American furniture company called Friendly Furniture Makers. The company has a team of sales analysts in their marketing department that need to analyze sales trends and forecast future sales so the manufacturing operation knows what to produce.

The company needs to convert a batch program that compares predicted and actual sales for a product to a Web report that the sales analyst team can run on-demand. Currently, the report is generated from an overnight batch process using a program that contains a SAS macro called MakeReport. MakeReport runs four times to create a report for each product line: Desk, Chair, Bed, and Sofa.

#6 SAS Macro code is easy to convert to a stored process because all of your variables are already present in the code.

Your assignment is to convert the existing batch program into a stored process that allows the sales analysts to run the stored process from the Web browser. The sales analyst can select the product line from a drop-down list, select Run, and generate the report on demand, as shown in the following figure. This prompt replaces the parameter that is used in the macro code.

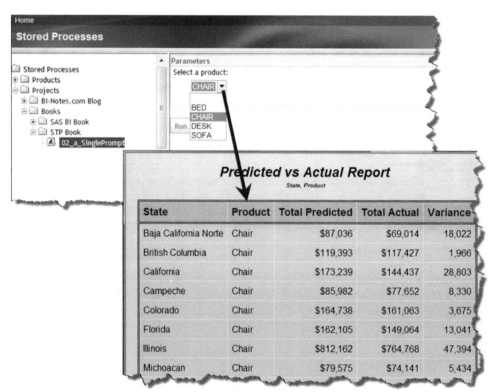

Figure 2-1 Using a single selection prompt

To convert this report, you must register a new stored process and add a single selection prompt for the product to the code. See Section 1.2, "Registering a Stored Process" for specific steps to register the stored process.

2.2.1 Creating a Single Prompt

As you register the stored process, create a text prompt with the name **prodprompt,** which allows a user to select a single item. This prompt contains a static list of the four product lines in our example. Figure 2-2 shows how to set up the prompt and how the resulting prompt appears in the Parameters tab.

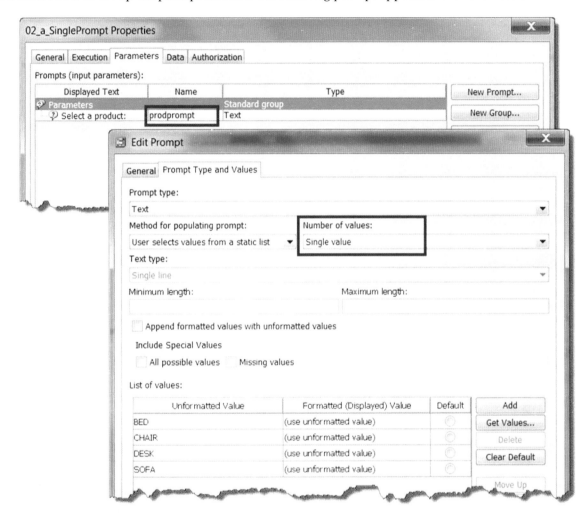

Figure 2-2 Creating a product prompt

2.2.2 Updating the Code

To modify the existing code, you must replace the current macro with the %STPBEGIN/%STPEND macros. The following code shows how to convert the existing legacy code to a stored process.

  #7 As your stored process code becomes more complex, ensure that your metadata descriptions and code comments explain what the code is doing and why.

Example 2-A Single Prompt	Required Modifications
~~%macro MakeReport(prodprompt);~~	Remove the macro statement. The code can run outside of the macro. The newly created prompt replaces the need for the macro parameter.
`libname booksamp meta library="STP Book Sample Data";`	Referencing the library via the META engine ensures that user credentials are used in authorizing access.

`proc sql;`
`create table work.qresult as`
`select distinct`
`  state label="State"`
`  ,propcase(product) as Product`
`    label="Product"`
`  ,sum(predict) as predictsum`
`    label="Total Predicted"`
`  format=dollar12.`
`  ,sum(actual) as actualsum`
`    label="Total Actual"`
`    format=dollar12.`
`  ,sum(predict)-sum(actual) as diff`
`  label="Variance"`
`    format=negparen10.`
`from booksamp.prdsal2011`
	Stored processes use the same BASE SAS code as other processes. No changes are required in the PROC SQL, which generates a temporary dataset that summarizes three variables by state and product.

`where upcase(product)` `   = "&prodprompt"`	Because you are converting this macro to a stored process, no code changes are required. As shown in Figure 2-1, the prompt name is prodprompt and is used here inside the double quotation marks. Use double quotation marks to ensure that the macro variable resolves correctly. If you use single quotes, SAS does not convert the &prodprompt macro variable, and the stored process will not return any results.

`group by state, product`
`order by state;`
`quit;`	

~~ods html file="//path/rpt_&prodprompt.xls";~~ `%stpbegin;`	The stored process returns the output to the Web browser so that you can remove the ODS HTML statements. The %STPBEGIN macro manages the output.

Example 2-A Single Prompt	Required Modifications
| ```
title1 "Predicted vs Actual Report";
title2 height=1 "State, Product";
proc print data=work.qresult label noobs;
run;
``` | PROC PRINT creates the final output from the temporary dataset. |
| ~~ods html close;~~
~~%mend;~~
%stpend; | Replace the macro end variable with the stored process end variable. |
| ~~%MakeReport(BED);~~
~~%MakeReport(CHAIR);~~
~~%MakeReport(DESK);~~
~~%MakeReport(SOFA);~~ | Delete the macro statements because the user executes the code when calling the stored process using the prompt to select the desired report. |

#8 After creating a stored process, test it by selecting several of the prompt choices to ensure that the user will get expected results.

2.3 Using Date Prompts

After successfully implementing the first report, the customer is pleased and wants additional changes. Because each analyst wanted to review different time periods, the old report contained several years of data. After seeing how easy it is to get quick results, the customer requests that you add a date filter to allow the sales analyst to select specific time periods.

You can make this change easily by adding a date range prompt and modifying the WHERE statement to include the new values for the prompt.

#9 When choosing the date prompts, use the Date Range prompt to provide users with the most flexibility when selecting time periods.

A date range prompt allows the user to select a broad date range. The prompt adds icons and a filter to assist the user. If unsure of the date, the user can select a specific day using the calendar icon. The user can even select relative dates, such as Yesterday or Beginning of current year from the date range drop-down lists.
```

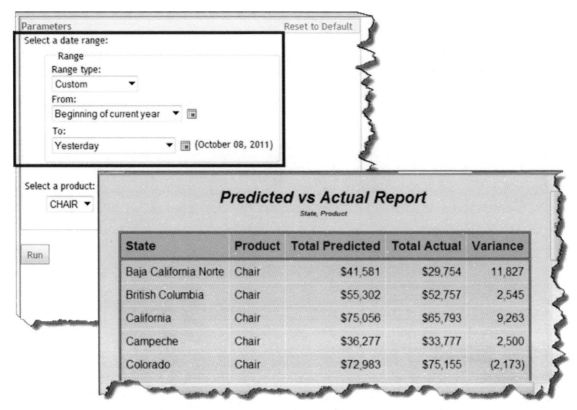

Figure 2-3 Using a date prompt with a stored process

2.3.1 Adding a Date Range Prompt

When registering the stored process, create a date range prompt called sale_date. The Parameters tab should contain two prompts, as shown in the following figure.

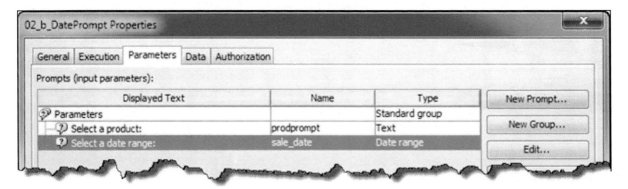

Figure 2-4 Adding a date range prompt

2.3.2 Understanding SAS Dates

Before updating the code, you must understand how SAS works with date variables. All date related prompts return values in the format DDMONYYYY, such as 24Apr2012.

When using a Date Range prompt, several automatic macro variables are created. The macro variables contain the minimum and maximum date range for the period. These values can be text or characters. For example, the sale_date prompt created in the last step would have two default macro variables that look like the following:

```
&sale_date_min = 01Jan2011
&sale_date_max = 07Oct2011
```

You can use these macro variables in the code to control the filtering or to display information to the user. For example, if you want to update the FOOTNOTE statement, use the macro variables as follows:

```
footnote1 height=1 "Programmed by BI-NOTES.COM  Sale Dates: &sale_date_min-
&sale_date_max";
```

Because these are character values, the code would translate in the report as the date value or any other text string as shown below:

Programmed by BI-NOTES.COM   Sale Dates: 01Jan2011 – 07Oct2011

However, when using prompt values within the code for filtering, those values must use proper SAS syntax to translate the text value into a valid SAS date value. To do this conversion place the text string inside double quotation marks and add the letter *d* as a suffix, such as "01Jan2011"d.

In a WHERE statement, you would need to use the two macro date variables as shown:

```
where "&sale_date_min"d <= date <= "&sale_date_max"d
```

The code is translated in the stored process as follows:

```
where "01Jan2011"d <= date <= "07Oct2011"d
```

2.3.3 Updating the Stored Process Code with Date Prompts

To update the code, you must add a new filter for the date range prompt.

Example 2-B Date Prompts	Required Modifications
| ```
libname booksamp meta library="STP Book Sample
Data";
proc sql;
create table work.qresult as
select distinct
  state
    label="State"
  ,propcase(product) as Product
    label="Product"
  ,sum(predict) as predictsum
    label="Total Predicted"
  format=dollar12.
  ,sum(actual) as actualsum
    label="Total Actual"
    format=dollar12.
  ,sum(predict)-sum(actual) as diff
  label="Variance"
    format=negparen10.
from booksamp.prdsal2011
where upcase(product)
  = "&prodprompt"
``` | |
| ```
AND "&sale_date_min"d
  <= date <=
"&sale_date_max"d
``` | The sale_date prompt uses the date range prompt type, therefore the WHERE statement is updated to filter based on the &sale_date_min and &sale_date_max automatic macro variables.

In the dataset, the date variable contains the sales date needed to filter the results. |
| ```
group by state, product
order by state
;
quit;
%stpbegin;
title1 'Predicted vs Actual Report';
title2 height=1 'State, Product';
proc print data=work.qresult label noobs;
run;
%stpend;
``` | |
```

2.4 Enabling a Multiple Selection Prompt

After adding the date prompt, the customer is impressed with the precise report data. Because the report data is more specific, the sales analysts want to select more than one product line at a time.

In the following figure, you can see how the modified stored process changes. The date range remains the same, but the Product prompt now allows multiple choices. In the results, note that the user selected Desk and Chair, which are in the report.

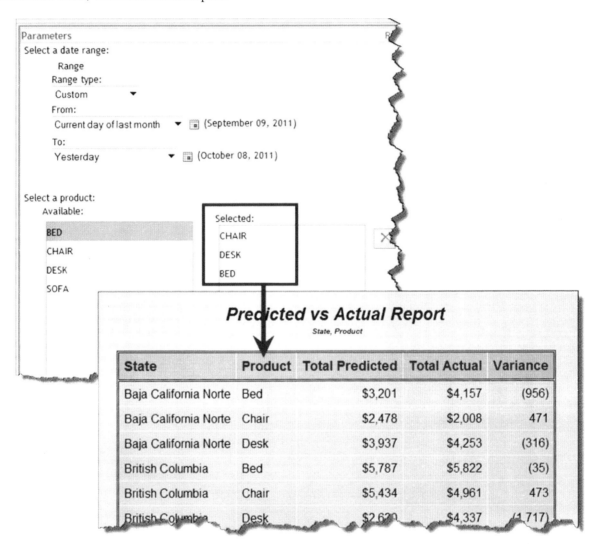

Figure 2-5 Adding multiple prompts to a stored process

Again, this task requires a quick modification to the existing prompt and code.

2.4.1 Converting a Single Selection Prompt

To convert a single selection prompt, return to your stored process and edit the prompt to allow users to select multiple values by following these steps:

1. From SAS Management Console, right-click the stored process and open the **Properties** window.

2. From the Parameters tab, select the **Select a product:** prompt text and select **Edit**.

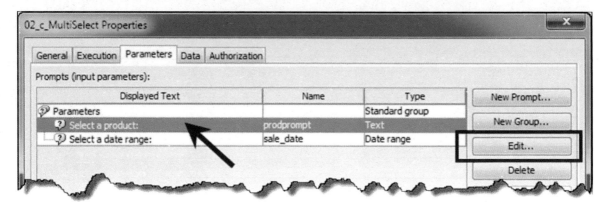

3. From the **Prompt Type and Values** tab, select **Multiple Values** from the Number of values drop-down box.

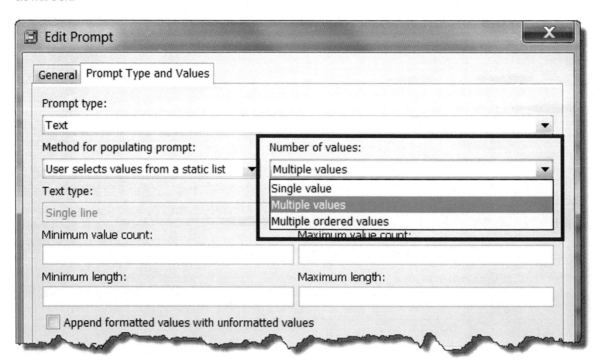

4. Select **OK** to exit the window and save your changes.

2.4.2 Modifying the Code for Multiple Values

After you modified the prompt, you must update the stored process code to control the number of user selections. The critical question is how will you know how many values the user selected?

When a prompt allows multiple values, it generates several additional automatic variables. These macro variables contain the user selections and the number of selections the user made. The following table shows the automatic variable name, provides a definition, and gives an example of the resulting macro name.

Automatic Macro Variable	Definition	Example
PROMPTNAME	The value of the prompt when one value is selected or the first value in a group of multiple selections.	*prodprompt*
PROMPTNAME_COUNT	The number of selections the user made.	*prodprompt_Count*
PROMPTNAME0	The number of selections the user made. Appears when multiple selections are available.	*prodprompt0*
PROMPTNAME1 ... PROMPT_NAMEN	Each user choice with a number. Appears when multiple selections are available.	*prodprompt1, prodprompt2, prodprompt3, prodprompt4*

Each stored process generates log information that contains the macro variables choices and results of the stored process execution. In Chapter 5, "Troubleshooting Stored Processes" you will learn more about accessing and reviewing the log.

The following table contains partial log information for a stored process that ran twice:

Example 1. User selects three values	Example 2. User selects one value
The user selected three product values: Bed, Chair, and Desk. This partial log contains six macro variables. PRODPROMPT_COUNT and PRODPROMPT0 are both set to three, indicating three values are available to process. The three values are numbered and contained in the PRODPROMPT*n* variables.	The user selected one value, Sofa. In that partial log, two macro variables are contained. As a result, the PRODPROMPT_COUNT indicates that the count, which is one and the PRODPROMPT contains the value (Sofa).

```
PRODPROMPT=BED                          PRODPROMPT=SOFA
PRODPROMPT0=3

PRODPROMPT1=BED
PRODPROMPT2=CHAIR
PRODPROMPT3=DESK

PRODPROMPT_COUNT=3                       PRODPROMPT_COUNT=1
```

#10 &*promptname1* - &*promptname(count)* automatic macro values are not created when only one value is selected therefore your code should account for that difference.

To ensure that the stored process can accommodate one value or four values, you must add a macro and some conditional coding to the WHERE statement.

Example 2-C Multi-Selection Prompt	Required Modifications
```%macro query;```	When the WHERE statement is updated, it requires macro language logic statements. You can use these statements in a macro program only. Add the code to start a macro called QUERY.

```libname booksamp meta library="STP Book Sample Data";```
```proc sql;```
```create table work.qresult as```
```select distinct state label="State"```
``` ,propcase(product) label="Product"```
``` ,sum(predict) as predictsum```
```   label="Total Predicted"```
```   format=dollar12.```
``` ,sum(actual) as actualsum```
```   label="Total Actual" format=dollar12.```
``` ,sum(predict)-sum(actual) as diff```
```   label="Variance" format=negparen10.```
```from booksamp.prdsal2011```	

```where upcase(product)```
~~```= "&PRODPROMPT"```~~
```in (%if &prodprompt_count=1```
``` %then %do;```
```   "&prodprompt"```
``` %end;```
``` %else %do i = 1 %to```
```   &prodprompt_count;```
```   "&&prodprompt&i."```
``` %end;```
```)```
	Modify the current coding to handle the multiple values.
	
	The %IF/%THEN/%ELSE macro statements allow the code to conditionally execute. In this situation, we are testing &prodprompt_count. if equals 1 then filter only on the &prodprompt. value.
	
	Otherwise, &prodprompt_count is greater than 1 so loop through the count and place each value in the WHERE statement. Notice that the double ampersands (&&) were added to decode the macro variable properly and there is no period between prodprompt and i.

```AND "&sale_date_min"d<=date<="&sale_date_max"d```
```group by state, product```
```order by state;```
```quit;```	

~~```%stpbegin;```~~
```title1 'Predicted vs Actual Report';```
```title2 height=1 'State, Product';```
```proc print data=work.qresult label noobs;```
```run;```
	Move %STPBEGIN to start after the macro ends.
	
	Place PROC PRINT inside the macro code.

```%mend query;```
```%stpbegin;```
```   %query;```
	Close the program macro with the %mend statement.
	
	Start the stored process output and call the program macro.

```%stpend;```	

Chapter

3

Making Decisions with Code

Use conditional SAS programming, in order for your stored process code to create output dynamically based on the user's selections. This allows for very flexible programming that can handle anything that the prompt framework can throw at it. In Chapter 2, "Creating Simple Stored Processes", you learned the basics of creating stored processes.

You can add macro language conditional logic to programs to increase the code flexibility and reduce the need for duplicated reports. In this chapter, you will learn to use conditional logic with optional prompts so that the user can select the final report contents. By using the stored process samples from Chapter 2, the same code instantly adapts to new requirements and overall maintenance is reduced.

3.1 Making a Prompt Optional

Our business scenario customer, Friendly Furniture Makers, has used the new stored process for several weeks with great results. To expand on that scenario, the customer called today with some new reporting requirements. Six months ago, they implemented a promotional campaign in the state of New York. They want to update that report with a state prompt that allows the sales analysts to select specific states when needed. However, they also want the option of including all states for other reports.

In Figure 3-1, the window on the top-left shows all states, while the window on the bottom-right shows results for New York only and does not contain a column for state. The heading provides more information about the user's selection. To update the report for this optional prompt, add a new text prompt called State and update the stored process code with conditional logic for the new prompt.

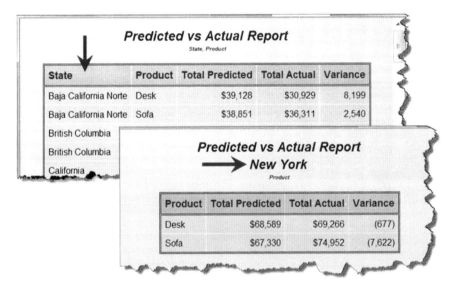

Figure 3-1 Different output from State Prompt

3.1.1 Adding an Optional Prompt

When creating a prompt, you can set the prompt type as required or optional. When a prompt is required, the stored process does not continue until the user selects a value. Alternatively, optional prompts do not require a response. In Chapter 2, "Creating Simple Sorted Processes" all of the prompts were optional. If a user submitted the report without selecting a product or date, the stored process would return a blank report because PROC SQL code would have returned a null value. The report is blank and confuses the user, thus, the user does not have a good stored process experience.

When adding the new prompt, create a Text prompt called State and ensure that the **Requires a non-blank value** checkbox is empty. If you need to create a required prompt, select the **Requires a non-blank value** checkbox.

In the following figure, you can see how the stored process window changes due to requiring the prompt. When the prompt is required, the user sees an asterisk (*) symbol before each of the required prompts. In this figure, the optional state prompt does not have an asterisk (*) symbol, which means that State is not required.

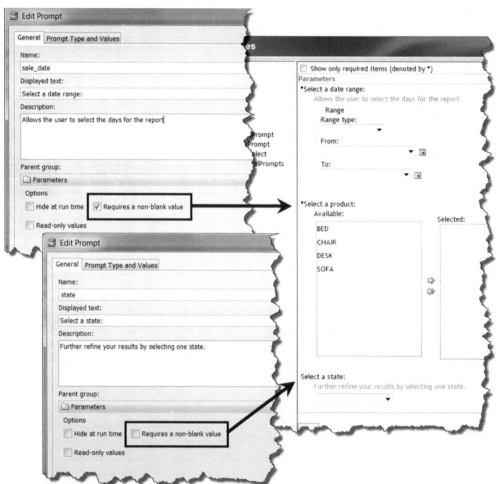

Figure 3-2 Using required and optional prompts

You must add an optional text prompt called State to Example 2-C Multi-Selection Prompt. Create the prompt to select a single selection from the State variables available from the data set, as explained in Section 2.2.1, "Creating a Single Prompt".

3.1.2 Modifying the Stored Process Code

Modify the code in Example 2-C Multi-Selection Prompt to add conditional logic that tests whether the State macro variable has a value and produces the correct output.

Example 3-A Optional Prompts	Required Modifications

``%macro query;
libname booksamp meta library="STP Book Sample Data";
proc sql; create table work.qresult as select distinct state label="State"
  ,propcase(product) as Product
    label="Product"
  ,sum(predict) as predictsum
    label="Total Predicted"
  format=dollar12.
  ,sum(actual) as actualsum
    label="Total Actual" format=dollar12.
  ,sum(predict)-sum(actual) as diff
    label="Variance" format=negparen10.
from booksamp.prdsal2011
  where "&sale_date_min"d
    <= date <= "&sale_date_max "d
and upcase(product) in
(%if &prodprompt_count = 1
%then %do; "&prodprompt" %end;
%else %do i = 1 %to
  &prodprompt_count;
    "&&prodprompt&i."
%end;)```
	No changes are required to the existing macro code.

```%if %length(&state) > 0 %then %do; and state = "&state" %end;```	Use conditional macro logic statements to test the length of the &state variable to determine if the user selected a value for the state prompt. When the variable length is greater than 0, the code inserts a filter for the state variable; otherwise, the filter is not applied.
```group by state, product order by state; quit; title1 'Predicted vs. Actual Report';```	

``%if %length(&state) = 0 %then %do;
  title2 height=1 'State, Product';
%end;
%else %do;
  title2 "&state";
  title3 height=1 'Product';
%end;```
	Use the same conditional logic to modify the TITLE statement. When the state prompt is empty, the length equals 0, causing the existing TITLE2 to appear.
	
	However, when a state is selected and the length is greater than 0, then the TITLE2 statement is replaced with the state name, and a TITLE3 is added to indicate that Product only is shown.

```proc print data=work.qresult label noobs;```	

``var
  %if %length(&state) = 0 %then %do;
    state
  %end;
product predictsum actualsum diff;```
	You can apply the conditional logic to the VAR statement in the PROC PRINT to control which variables appear in the report. When state is empty, the state column appears in the report.

Example 3-A Optional Prompts	Required Modifications

```
run;
%mend query;
%stpbegin;
  %query;
%stpend;
```

3.2 Adding Prompt Groups

After the customer saw the different reports based on state selection, the customer had more ideas for improving their stored processes.

The sales analysts want to include an optional graph with the report, but they cannot agree on graph type or which variable to plot. What if we allow the users choose if they want a graph to appear and if so, allow them to select the variable for the chart?

Consider this example, if the sales analyst selects **Yes** for **Include a graph?** prompt, the other two prompts appear for the graph type and variable to plot. In the modified stored process, shown in the following figure the sales analyst requested a pie chart based on the Actual Sales variable. To modify the stored process, create a prompt group with a Chart Type and Variable prompts and update the stored process code.

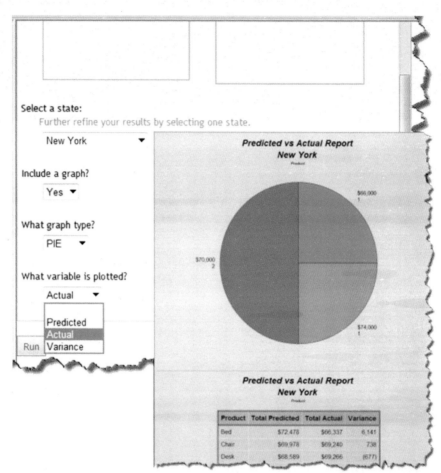

Figure 3-3 Different output from State Prompt

3.2.1 Creating a Prompt Group

Prompt groups are a unique prompt type because they control and contain other prompts. In Figure 3-2, when the user selects **Yes** from the **Include a graph?** drop-down list, the two other prompts appear and provide the options for chart type and variable. When setting up the group prompt, you create the Allow two choices (Yes and No) group prompt and then associate selection-dependent prompts (Graph Type and Variable) with the Yes choice.

To create prompt group, complete the following steps:

1. In the SAS Management Console, modify the stored process that you want to update.

2. From the Parameters tab, select the **New Group** button to create the new prompt group.

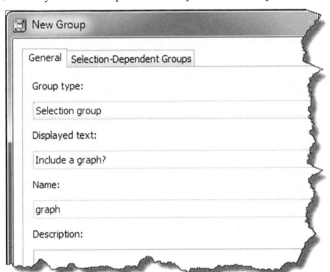

   a. In the **Group type** drop-down, select **Selection group**. This allows you to enter selection values and make the group optionally appear.

   b. In the **Displayed text** field, type **Include a graph?** The user sees this value.

   c. In the **Name** field, type a name for the prompt, such as **Graph**. This is the macro variable used in the code.

3. From the Selection-Dependent Groups tab, add the two selection values (Yes and No).

   a. Select the **New Group** button. In the **Displayed Text** and **Value** fields, type **Yes**. Select **OK**.

   b. Repeat step a. Type **No** for the value.

   c. In the Default column, select the radio button for **No**. As the customer requested, the graph option is off by default. When you select this option, it prevents the associated prompts from displaying unless the user selects the Yes option.

   d. Select **OK** to close the New Group window.

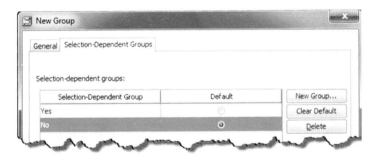

   When the main Prompt window appears, you can see your new Include a graph? group with the Yes and No choices.

4. Create two new prompts, GraphType and Variable. When the user selects the Yes option, you want these two new prompts to appear.

Follow these steps to set up the prompt:

a. Select the row Yes to highlight it blue then select New Prompt.

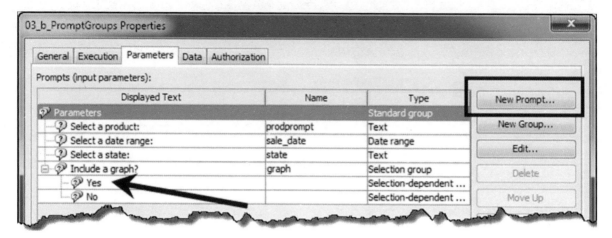

b. Create a text prompt called GraphType that allows the user to select a value from a static list. The value list is HBAR, PIE, and PLOT.

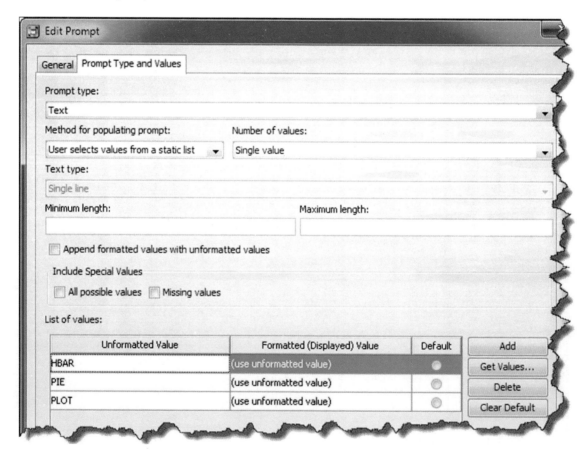

c. Create a text prompt called Variable that allows the user to select a value from a static list. The choices are the variables created in the stored process PROC SQL step: predictsum, actualsum, and diff.

d. Because the variable names are not business-friendly, update the **Formatted (Displayed) Value** column to a term that helps the user, such as **diff** becomes **Variance**.

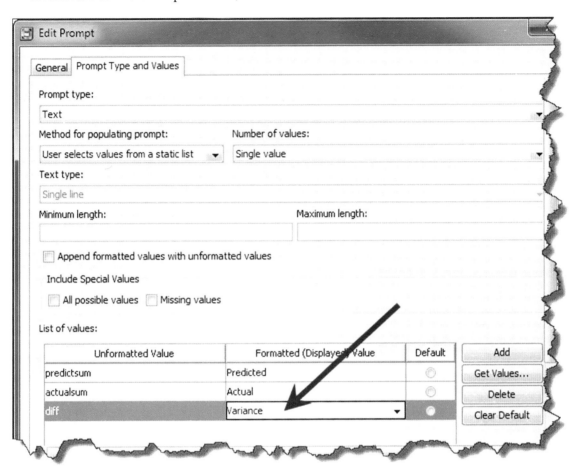

5. After creating the prompts you need, review the Parameters tab to ensure that the prompt group contains the correct options. There is a new group prompt called Include a graph? that has two possible selections, Yes and No. Depending on the Yes answer, there are two available prompts: What graph type? and What variable is plotted?

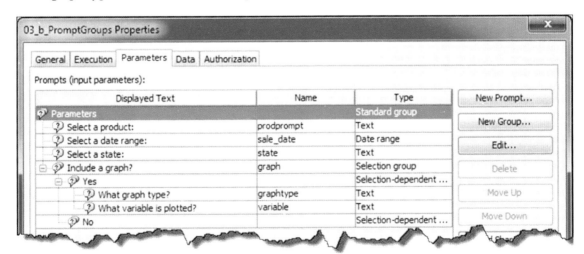

3.2.2 Updating the Stored Process Code

After the prompts are available, you need to update the code to work with the three new prompt values and add the code for the graph types. Using conditional macro logic, you can easily manage the choices.

 #11 **Use prompt groups with conditional macro code to increase the flexibility and reach of stored processes.**

Example 3-B Prompt Groups	Required Modifications

```%macro query;```
 ```libname booksamp meta library="STP Book Sample Data";```
 ```proc sql; create table work.qresult as select distinct state```
 ```   label="State"```
 ``` ,propcase(product) as Product```
 ```   label="Product"```
 ``` ,sum(predict) as predictsum```
 ```   label="Total Predicted"```
 ```format=dollar12.```
 ``` ,sum(actual) as actualsum```
 ```   label="Total Actual" format=dollar12.```
 ``` ,sum(predict)-sum(actual) as diff```
 ```   label="Variance" format=negparen10.```
 ```from booksamp.prdsal2011```
 ``` where "&sale_date_min"d```
 ```   <= date <= "&sale_date_max "d```
 ```and upcase(product) in```
 ```(%if &prodprompt_count = 1```
 ```%then %do; "&prodprompt" %end;```
 ```%else %do i = 1 %to```
 ``` &prodprompt_count;```
 ```   "&&prodprompt&i."```
 ```%end;)```
 ```%if %length(&state) > 0 %then %do;```
 ``` and state = "&state"```
 ```%end;```
 ```group by state, product```
 ```order by state```
 ```quit;```
 ```title1 'Predicted vs Actual Report';```
 ```%if %length(&state) = 0 %then %do;```
 ``` title2 height=1 'State, Product';```
 ```%end;```
 ```%else %do;```
 ``` title2 "&state"```
 ``` title3 height=1 'Product';```
 ```%end;```
	No changes are needed to this code.

```%if "&graph" = "Yes" %then %do;```
 ``` %if "&graphtype" = "PLOT"```
 ```   %then %do;```
 ```   proc &graphtype data=work.qresult;```
 ```   &graphtype &variable*product;```
	The **Include a graph?** prompt group was named **Graph,** which returns a Yes or No value. When the &Graph variable is Yes, this code builds a graph.
	
	 You must place the &GraphType macro

Example 3-B Prompt Groups	Required Modifications

``
  run; quit;
%end;
%else %do;
  proc gchart data=work.qresult;
  &graphtype &variable;
  run; quit;
  %end;
%end;
``
	variable in quotes when comparing the results. When used elsewhere in the code, the quotes are not required.
	
	Based on the result of the &GraphType and &Variable prompts, the code creates the appropriate graph.
	
	Use macro variables instead of hard coding to maintain flexible code. When adding variables in the future, the code easily accommodates the change.

```
proc print data=work.qresult label noobs;
var
  %if %length(&state) = 0 %then %do;
    state
  %end;
    product predictsum actualsum diff;
run;
%mend query;
%stpbegin;
  %query;
%stpend;
```

3.3 Chaining Reports

As the sales analysts use this report, they often return to other tools (for example, SAS Enterprise Guide) to review the specific raw data. To improve productivity, the analysts want to know if you can link each row from the summary report to a detail report that contains the raw data for the predicted and actual numbers.

This summary report would contain a drill-down detailed report that provides the exact data for each line. In the following figure, the original report is shown on the left, which is a summary report with the URL links listed for each record. After selecting the Detailed Report link, the user can view the Detail Report. In this example, the Detail Report is for the first row of the summary report. The Detail Report shows the specific dates for each record that is a part of the summary line.

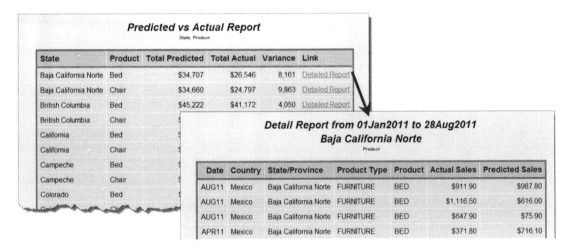

Figure 3-4 Creating a linking or chained report

3.3.1 Creating a Detailed Report

The Detail Report in Figure 3-4 is created from the Example 3-A Optional Prompts stored process code. When registering the stored process in the SAS Management Console, you can hide this stored process from users to ensure the report is only available from the summary report. This ensures that no user navigates to this stored process from a metadata folder view.

Note: Example 3-C Sales Detail is called *Sales Detail* so it can be linked to as shown in the examples.

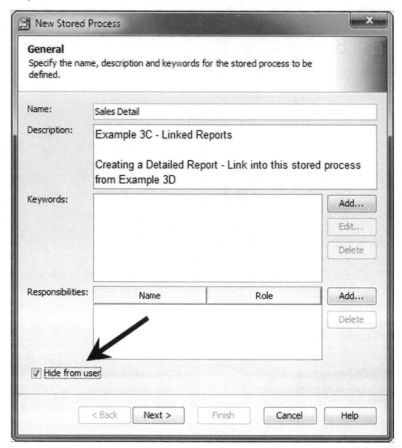

Figure 3-5 Hiding a stored process

 #12 Use the *Hide from user* checkbox to create and register stored processes that are available directly using a URL but should not be viewable in SAS Enterprise Guide or Web Stored Process Application listings. Use this method in chained stored processes where only the parent stored process should be viewable.

Use a copy of the summary report code in Example 3-A Optional Prompts, to make the following code changes in order to display all rows and variables. The new stored process only needs the sale_date, prodprompt, and state prompts.

Example 3-C Sales Detail	Required Modifications

```%macro query;```
```libname booksamp meta library="STP Book Sample Data";```
```proc sql;```
```create table work.qresult as select```	

~~Distinct~~ ~~state label="State",~~ ~~propcase(product) as product label="Product",~~ ~~sum(predict) as predictsum label="Total Predicted" format=dollar12.,~~	Remove the variables and calculations and replace with an asterisk (*) symbol to select all variables within the data table

Example 3-C Sales Detail	Required Modifications
~~sum(actual) as actualsum label="Total Actual"~~ ~~format=dollar12.,~~ ~~sum(predict)-sum(actual) as diff~~ ~~label="Variance" format=negparen10.~~ *	
| ```
from booksamp.prdsal2011
where "&sale_date_min"d <= date <=
"&sale_date_max"d
and upcase(product) in
``` | |
| ~~(%if &prodprompt_count = 1~~
~~%then %do;~~
    ("&prodprompt")
~~%end;~~
~~%else %do i = 1 %to~~
~~&prodprompt_count;~~
      ~~"&&prodprompt&i."~~
~~%end;)~~ | Each row in the table only corresponds to one product; remove the code for selecting multiple values.

Remove everything except the "&prodprompt" statement because this is needed to work with the prompt. |
| ```
%if %length(&state) > 0 %then %do;
  and state = "&state"
%end;
``` | |
| ~~group by state, product~~ | Remove the group by state so that the query returns all records. |
| ```
order by state;
quit;
``` | |
| ```
title1 "Detail Report from &SALE_DATE_MIN to
&SALE_DATE_MAX ";
``` <br>~~%if %length(&state) = 0 %then %do;~~<br>  ~~title2 height=1 'State, Product';~~<br>~~%end;~~<br>~~%else %do;~~<br>  `title2 "&state";`<br>  `title3 height=1 'Product';`<br>~~%end;~~ | Add the Sale Date macro variables to the TITLE statement.<br><br>Because the state variable is included in each row of the summary report, remove the conditional logic for the different TITLE statements. |
| ```
proc print data=work.qresult label noobs;
``` | |
| `Var`<br>~~%if %length(&state) = 0 %then %do;~~<br>  ~~state~~<br>~~%end;~~<br>~~product predictsum actualsum diff~~<br>```
date country state product actual
predict;
``` | Modify the list of variables included in the result window so that it reflects the available variables in the raw data query results. |
| ```
run;
%mend query;
%stpbegin;
  %query;
%stpend;
``` | |

3.3.2 Updating the Summary Report with a URL

To link to the Sales Detail stored process from the summary stored processes requires that you understand how the parameters are included in the URL path. URLs include the program name and can include input parameters that can correspond to the selected prompts.
```

Understanding URL Paths

To access the stored process by the URL path, you must know the stored process path and program name. In the following figure, you can see how the Web browser locates the stored process path and program name. After the **http://MachineName:PortNumber/SASStoredProcess/do?**, the _program variable completes the URL path for the stored process. The plus sign (+) replaces spaces in the path.

Figure 3-6 Program path in the Web browser

The specific prompt (and macro variables) are included after the &_program parameter. As shown in the following figure, the URL passes all four prompt values to the stored process. An ampersand (&) symbol appears between each input parameter.

- &sale_date_min=01Jan2011
- &sale_date_max=08Oct2011
- &prodprompt=CHAIR
- &state=British Columbia

Figure 3-7 Marco variables in the Web browser

The URL path method has limitations. Web browsers typically limit the URL field length and truncate any remaining values, which can cause unexpected results. There are ways around this limitation, which are covered in Chapter 11, "Generating Custom Output". For this example, there are few parameters and the approach works.

Building a URL path for the Stored Process

To build the URL, you must combine the program path and prompt values in an HTML hyperlink (<a>) tag. You need to build this URL string for each record in the temporary dataset. When the summary report appears in the Web browser, the HTML tag appears as a hyperlink as shown in Figure 3-4. The hyperlink already contains the exact path to pass to the URL. In the SAS Stored Process code, the URL path is programmed as follows:

"http://&_srvname:&_srvport/SASStoredProcess/do?%NRSTR(&_program)=&_metafolder.Sales+Detail%NRSTR(&sale_date_min)=&sale_date_min
%NRSTR(&sale_date_max)=&sale_date_max%NRSTR(&prodprompt)="||strip(product)
||%nrstr(&state)="||strip(state)

#13 For stored processes run through the web, use &_SRVNAME and &_SRVPORT reserved macro variables in the URL to avoid modifications if servers change. For non-web clients (such as SAS Enterprise Guide or SAS Add-in to MS Office) &_srvname and &_srvport must be defined as they are not automatically available from these locations.

When building the URL, several SAS functions and automatic variables can make the job easier. When inserting variables, you must use the concatenate (||) symbol to join values and the STRIP() function to remove any trailing blanks from the value. Macros are automatically resolved in SAS code when using double quotes; thus, in the example shown below you must use %NRSTR to prevent the &prompt_names variable from resolving before the URL string runs.

Reserved macros &_srvname, &_srvport, and &_metafolder are used. This ensures that the program code is portable between metadata folders and machines, which is extremely useful when moving the stored process from Development to Production environments.

#14 Register all of your chained stored processes in the same metadata folder so that you can use the &_METAFOLDER reserved macro in your URL.

The main differences in the detailed report are that one allows all records and one includes the new URLLink variable. Use a copy of the report code in Example 3-B Prompt Groups

Example 3-D Linked Reports	Required Modifications

```%macro query;```
```libname booksamp meta library="STP Book Sample Data";```
```proc sql; create table work.qresult as select distinct```
```state label="State"```
``` ,propcase(product) as Product label="Product"```
``` ,sum(predict) as predictsum```
```   label="Total Predicted"   format=dollar12.```
``` ,sum(actual) as actualsum```
```   label="Total Actual" format=dollar12.```
``` ,sum(predict)-sum(actual) as diff```
``` label="Variance" format=negparen10.```	

```,"<a href='http://&_srvname:&_srvport```
``` /SASStoredProcess/do?```
``` %NRSTR(&_program)=```
```&_metafolder.Sales+Detail```
``` %NRSTR(&sale_date_min)=&sale_date_min```
``` %NRSTR(&sale_date_max)=&sale_date_max```
``` "||"```
``` %NRSTR(&prodprompt)="||STRIP(product)```
``` ||"%NRSTR(&state)=```
``` "||STRIP(state)||"'>```
``` Detailed Report</a>"```
``` as URLLink label="Link"```
	Add a variable called URLLink to the PROC SQL table.
	
	The URL is embedded with hyperlink (<a href=> </a>) tags. In the report, the users see a hyperlink called *Detailed Report*. The underlying code points to the detailed report stored process.
	
	Note: This example is spaced so you can see how to code the URL.

```from booksamp.prdsal2011``` ```where "&sale_date_min"d <= date <= "&sale_date_max"d```	

Example 3-D Linked Reports	Required Modifications

```
and upcase(product) in
(%if &prodprompt_count = 1
 %then %do;
    "&prodprompt"
 %end;
 %else %do i = 1 %to
 &prodprompt_count;
    "&&prodprompt&i."
 %end;  )
%if %length(&state) > 0 %then %do;
  and state = "&state"
%end;
group by state, product
order by state;
quit;
title1 'Predicted vs Actual Report';
%if %length(&state) = 0 %then %do;
  title2 height=1 'State, Product';
%end;
%else %do;
  title2 "&state";
  title3 height=1 'Product';
%end;
%if "&graph" = "Yes" %then %do;
  %if "&graphtype" = "PLOT" %then %do;
  proc &graphtype data=work.qresult;
   &graphtype &variable*product;
  run; quit;
  %end;
  %else %do;
  proc gchart data=work.qresult;
   &graphtype &variable;
  run; quit;
  %end;
%end;
proc print data=work.qresult label noobs;
var
  %if %length(&state) = 0 %then %do;
      state
  %end;
product predictsum actualsum diff
```

`URLLink;`	Add the new variable.

```
run;
%mend query;
%stpbegin;
  %query;
%stpend;
```

Chapter

4

Controlling Output Options

In previous chapters, you learned how to create stored processes, add optional prompts, and add a graph to the report. Many implementations start with functionality, but improving the view is typically the next request from users. Analytical results are paramount to success; however, appearances matter when displaying the graphs and reports as it affects a user's impression of the entire system.

In this chapter, you will learn how to use different style sheets to change your stored process appearance, work with different graphic device types, and add a drill-down link to a chart.

4.1 Changing the Appearance of Your Output

SAS provides more than 40 different style sheets to customize your stored processes appearance. The style sheets lets you change fonts, colors, and background images for the reports, charts, and tables. In the following figure, we ran a stored process using four different style sheets. The same report has different colors, fonts, and overall appearance. You can also create or add your own customized style sheets. Refer to the SAS Support site for more information about customized style sheets.

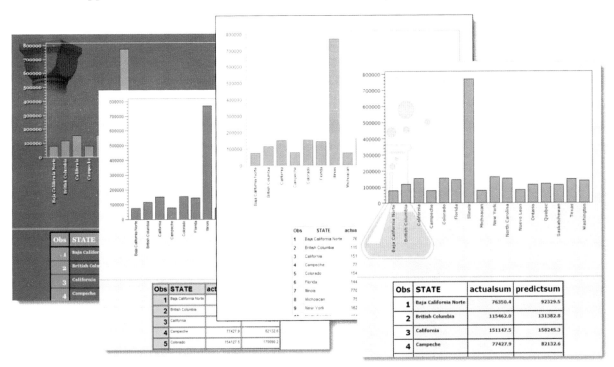

Figure 4-1 Applying style sheets to stored processes

The SAS system offers several reserved macros available for your use. Change the _ODSSTYLE reserved macro value to control which style sheet your stored process uses. This reserved macro can also be set from a prompt so that the user can decide at run time how the report should appear. Adding this prompt does not require any code changes.

4.1.1 Setting the Stored Process Style

Create a new prompt in the stored process named _ODSSTYLE, and include the style sheet name in the default value box.

1. From the SAS Management Console, select the stored process to modify and navigate to the **Parameters** tab.

2. Create a text prompt named _ODSSTYLE. You must use the reserved macro name to ensure the change occurs.

3. In some cases, you might not want the user to change the style sheet. To prevent the prompt from displaying, select the **Hide at run time** checkbox.

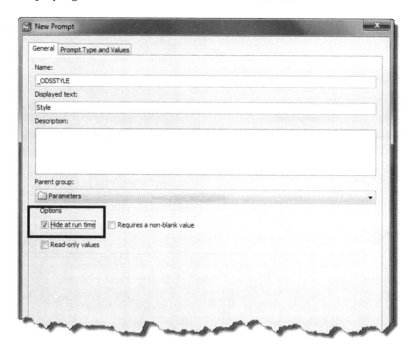

4. In the **Prompt Type and Values** tab, add the style sheet name to the Default Value field. The SASWEB style uses a white background with blue text.

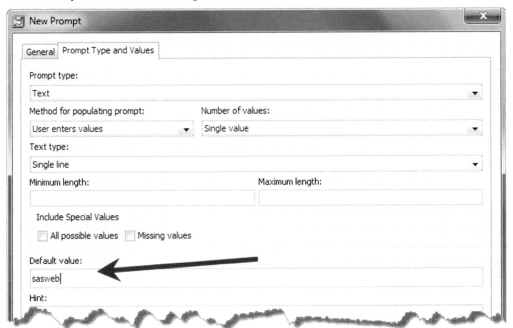

5. Select **OK** to create the prompt.

6. Run the stored process to review the change.

4.1.2 Using a Default Style Prompt

As an alternative to creating a style sheet prompt, you can use a SAS-provided shared prompt. Use the following steps to add a shared prompt to your stored process.

1. From the SAS Management Console, select a stored process to modify.

2. From the **Parameters** tab, select **Add Shared**.

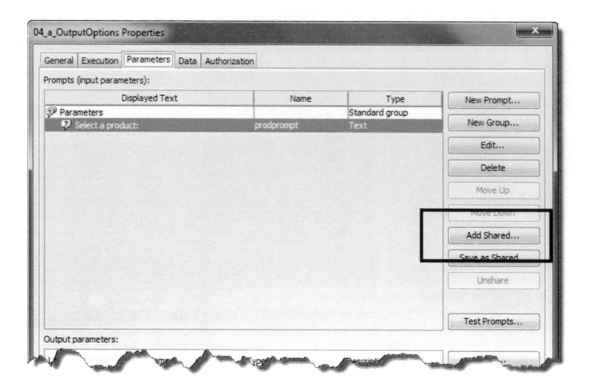

3. From the Products>SAS Intelligence Platform>Samples folder, select one of ODS Styles prompts, such as ODS Styles-Static.

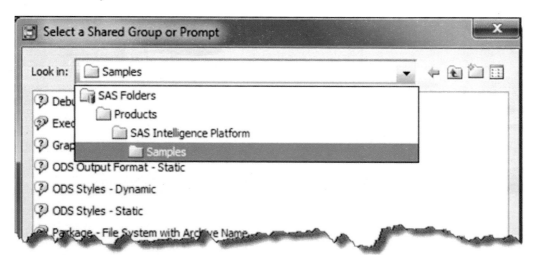

4. When prompted to change the prompt name, select **OK** to keep the current value. The prompt name _OdsStyle corresponds to the reserved macro variable.

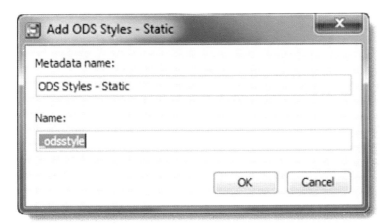

5. Because this is a shared prompt, you cannot make any changes until it is no longer shared. Select the prompt, select **Unshare**.

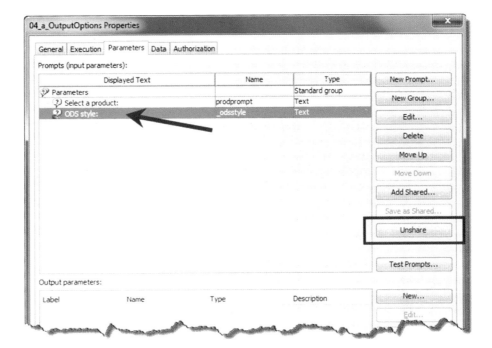

6. When the shared prompt is unshared, the system copies it to the stored process. The system displays a confirmation message to ensure this is what you want to do, select **Yes** to continue.

7. You can edit this prompt to set a default style or to hide the prompt.

   If you decide not to use the **Hide at run time** option, report users can select one of _odsstyle values, as shown in the following figure.

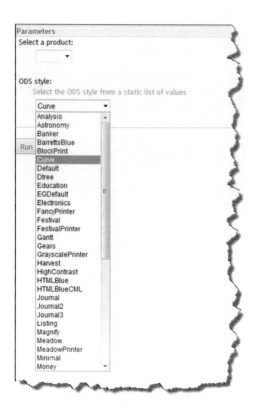

4.1.3 Changing the Stored Process Graphics Output

When exporting a stored process to multiple formats, such as HTML, RTF, or PDF, the user might need more flexibility for the graphics output. For instance, ActiveX or Java charts might work on a Web browser but not display as well in a PDF file. As with ODSSTYLE, you can use the _GOPT_DEVICE reserved macro to control the graphics device.

#15   **In the Samples folder, the shared prompt group Execution Options includes prompts for _GOPT_DEVICE , _ODSDEST , _ODSSTYLE, and _DEBUG.**

Follow the same steps to add the shared prompt for _ODSSTYLE to add the shared Graphics Device prompt that allows users to set the graphic device used.

Figure 4-2 Graphic output options

Working with ActiveX Graphics

In SAS 9.3, the default graphic format for SAS graphs for HTML and RTF output formats is PNG. Similar to JPG or TIFF, PNG has a smaller file size, supports more colors, and uses the transparency functionality. Some graphic devices can provide functionality to the user without requiring changes to the stored process code. This is useful when one report does not completely meet everyone's needs but the user can changed it immediately before printing or copying into a presentation.

The ActiveX device driver offers a right-click menu that allows users to change the graph type, appearance, legends, titles, and so on. In the following figure, we changed the graph type and style sheet for the output.

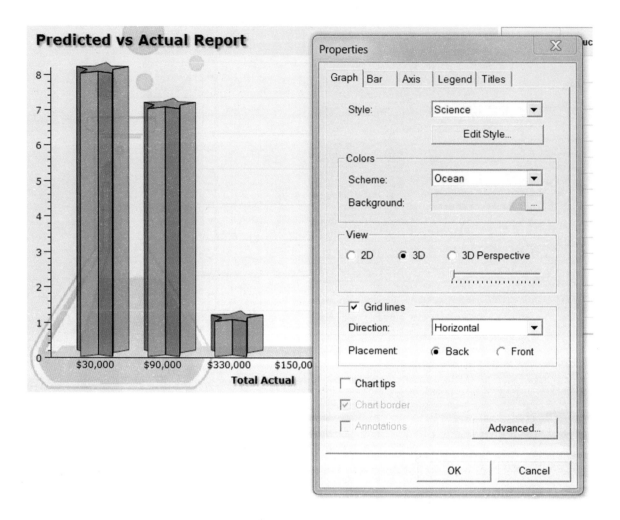

Figure 4-3 ActiveX Right-Click Menu

The ActiveX device driver is a locally installed product. If the users do not have SAS/GRAPH installed on their computers, they must install the device driver. To automate this process partially, add the following code to any stored processes using graph in ACTIVEX format:

```
%let _odsoptions=codebase="/sasweb/graph/sasgraph.exe";
```

Because a local installation might not possible in all organizations, another option is to make the stored process use the ActiveX Image option. Add the following code statement to set the graphics device to this format:

```
%let _gopt_device=ACTXIMG;
```

#16 You can enable ActiveX graphics by adding the reserved macro variable _ODSOPTIONS, and then point the CODEBASE to the loaded sasgraph.exe widget. Add this line to your code:
   %let _odsoptions=codebase="/sasweb/graph/sasgraph.exe";

4.2 Changing the Stored Process Layout

In Section 3.2, "Adding Prompt Groups" the stored process added an optional graph to the output. After scrolling to review results, the customer has asked if there is a way to see the graph and table side-by-side. The analysts like the graphical information and asked that graph always be included, but the user can still select the type of graph and the variable that is plotted.

The modified stored process should resemble the following figure. The graph appears on the left and the table on the right. This figure uses the Statistical style sheet.

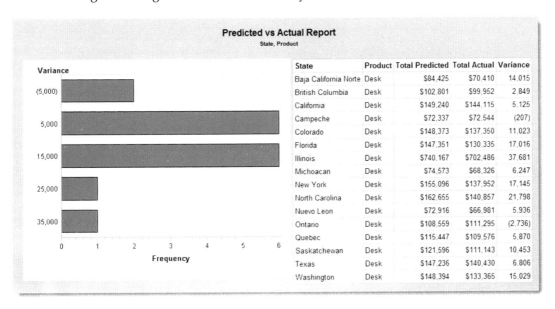

Figure 4-4 Side-by-side layout

4.2.1 Removing Grouped Prompts

You must modify the prompts so that users cannot choose to include the graph, as it is always available. Delete the Graph prompt, and move the GraphType and Variable prompts.

1. From the SAS Management console, select the stored process you want to modify.

2. In the Parameters tab, select the first prompt under the Yes option and select **Edit**, as shown in the following figure.

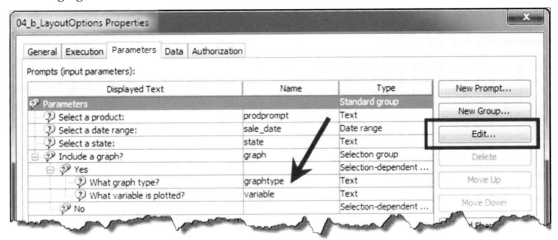

3. In the Parent group drop-down, select **Parameters**. This controls where the prompt is located.

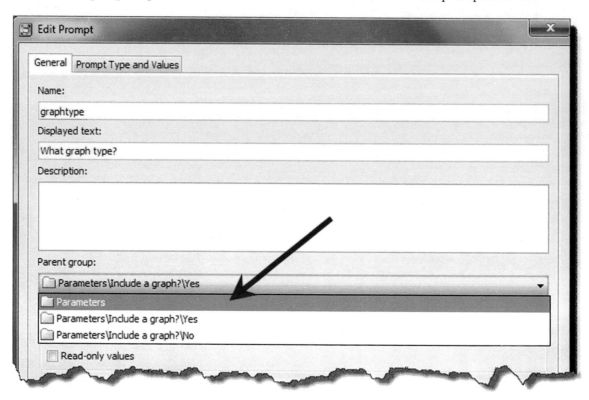

4. Repeat steps 2 and 3 so that the Variable prompt is part of the Parameters group.

5. Select the Include a graph? group and select **Delete** to remove the group prompt.

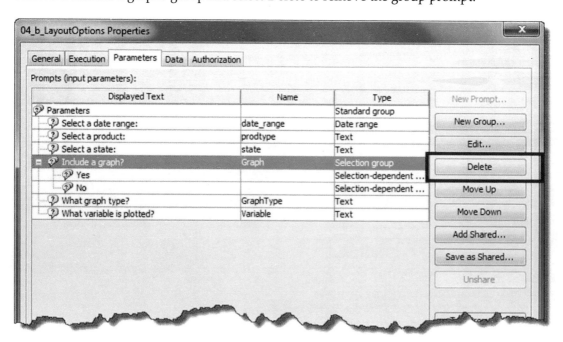

When using the stored process, the users no longer see the Include a graph? Option but they can still select What graph type? and What variable is plotted?.

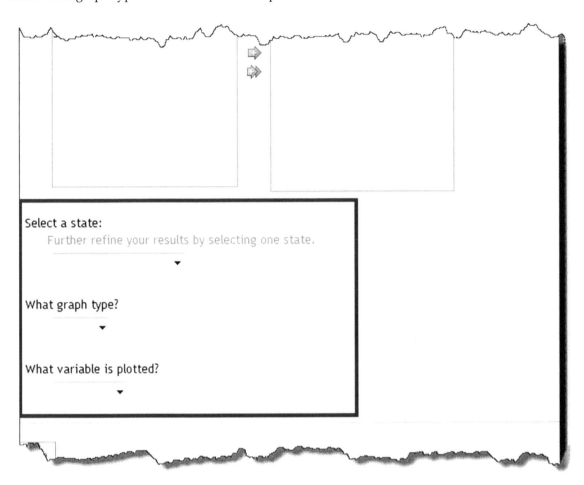

Select a state:
   Further refine your results by selecting one state.
                                        ▼

What graph type?
            ▼

What variable is plotted?
               ▼

4.2.2 Updating the Code

In order that the report can print the results side-by-side, the code needs to use additional options. ODS LAYOUT, experimental in releases SAS 9.1.3 to 9.3, allows you to define and assign each output element into specific regions or columns.

Example 4-B Layout Options	Required Modifications
| ```
%macro query;
libname booksamp meta library="STP Book
Sample Data";
proc sql; create table work.qresult as select
distinct state
   label="State"
 ,propcase(product) as Product
   label="Product"
 ,sum(predict) as predictsum
   label="Total Predicted"
 format=dollar12.
 ,sum(actual) as actualsum
   label="Total Actual" format=dollar12.
``` | No changes are required to this code. |
```

Example 4-B Layout Options	Required Modifications

```
   ,sum(predict)-sum(actual) as diff
     label="Variance" format=negparen10.
from booksamp.prdsal2011
  where "&sale_date_min"d
    <= date <= "&sale_date_max "d
and upcase(product) in
(%if &prodprompt_count = 1
%then %do; "&prodprompt" %end;
%else %do i = 1 %to
  &prodprompt_count;
    "&&prodprompt&i."
%end;)
%if %length(&state) > 0 %then %do;
  and state = "&state"
%end;
group by state, product
order by state;
quit;

title1 'Predicted vs Actual Report';
%if %length(&state) = 0 %then %do;
  title2 height=1 'State, Product';
%end;
%else %do;
  title2 "&state";
  title3 height=1 'Product';
%end;
```

```ods layout start columns=2;```
 	
```ods region;```
	Open the ODS LAYOUT functionality and set the Columns option to 2. Add an ODS REGION to place the graph in the first column.

~~%if "&graph" = "Yes" %then %do;~~	This %IF/%THEN conditional logic was here to support the prompt group. With the Graph group prompt removed, delete this code and the matching %END statement.

```
  %if "&graphtype" = "PLOT" %then %do;
  proc &graphtype data=work.qresult;
   &graphtype &variable*product;
  run; quit;
  %end;
  %else %do;
  proc gchart data=work.qresult;
   &graphtype &variable;
  run; quit;
  %end;
```

~~%end;~~	Remove the matching %END statement for the %IF/%THEN statement above.
```ods region;```	Add the ODS REGION to indicate the table belongs in the second column. You do not need to add any code to end or close the ODS REGION.

Example 4-B Layout Options	Required Modifications
| ```
proc print data=work.qresult label noobs;
var
  %if %length(&state) = 0 %then %do;
    state
  %end;
    product predictsum actualsum diff;
run;
``` | |
| `ods layout end;` | Close the ODS LAYOUT statement. |
| ```
%mend query;
%stpbegin;
  %query;
%stpend;
``` | |

4.3 Linking from Graphs

Linking between different reports, as shown in Section 3.3, "Chaining Reports" is a matter of building a URL string that links to a detailed report. However, some of this capability built in to the SAS graph procedure. This allows users to interact by drilling-down for further results. As shown in the following figure, the user clicked the orange bar representing the sales of desks in Illinois in order to review the detailed report that only includes records related to that information.

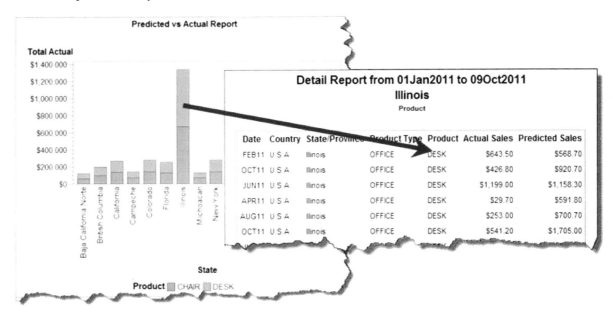

Figure 4-5 Drill-down chart example

#17 See the SAS GRAPH documentation for more examples of using ODS options within the graphics output.

Creating the URLlink in the data is similar to the example built previously in Section 3.3 "Chaining Reports" however, the <a> </a> HTML tags are not needed. PROC GRAPH has an HTML option available that can be used with the URLlink variable.

#18   Use the HTML_LEGEND= option to create a drill path from the legend itself.

In the following example, this code creates a bar chart that links to the Sale Detail report used in Chapter 3, "Making Decisions with Code". This code is similar to the code used in Section 2.4, "Enabling a Multiple Selection Prompt" in that it uses the same data table and variables.

Example 4-C Linked Graph	Required Modifications

```%macro query;```
```libname booksamp meta library="STP Book Sample Data";```
```proc sql;```
```create table qresult as select```
```distinct state label="State",```
``` product label="Product"```
	Code uses the same data table but the bar chart only needs the state, product, and actualsum variables.

```,sum(predict) as predictsum``` ``` label="Total Predicted" format=dollar12.```	Remove this code.
```sum(actual) as actualsum``` ```label="Total Actual" format=dollar12.,```	
```sum(predict) sum(actual) as diff``` ``` label="Variance" format=negparen10.,```	Remove this code

```"href='http://&_srvname:&_srvport/SASStoredProcess/do?```
```%nrstr(&_program)=```
```&_metafolder.Sales+Detail```
```%nrstr(&sale_date_min)=&sale_date_min%nrstr(&sale_date```
```_max)=&sale_date_max"```
```||"%nrstr(&prodprompt)="||strip(product)||"%nrstr(&sta```
```te)="||strip(state)||"'"```
```as URLLink label="Link"```
	This is the same URL used in Chapter 3, "Making Decisions with Code". It links to the same report.

```from booksamp.prdsal2011```
```where "&sale_date_min"d <= date <= "&sale_date_max"d```
```and   product in```
```(%if &prodprompt_count = 1```
``` %then %do;```
```   "&prodprompt"```
``` %end;```
``` %else %do i = 1 %to```
``` &prodprompt_count;```
```   "&&prodprompt&i."```
``` %end;```
```)```
``` group by state;```
```quit;```	

```title1 'Predicted vs Actual Report';```
```proc gchart data=work.qresult;```
``` vbar state /discrete subgroup=product```
```html=urlLink```
```   sumvar=actualsum;```
```run; quit;```
	Use a bar chart to plot the temporary dataset.
	
	Add the HTML option to allow the drill-down based on the URLlink variable. The GCHART procedure implements the rest of the process.

```%mend query;```
```%STPBEGIN;```
```%query;```
```%STPEND;```	

Chapter

5

Troubleshooting Stored Processes

If you have done any SAS coding, you appreciate the value of the log. The log contains a play-by-play account of how the program executed. When a stored process does not return the expected results, you can use the log to understand what happened.

This chapter explains where to find the stored process logs, how to use the URL to see the log during run time in the web browser and addresses some common errors.

5.1 Using the SAS Stored Process Web Application

All of the examples in the book thus far have used the SAS Stored Process Web application to view the stored process output. Use this case-sensitive path to access the page:

`http://MachineName:PortNumber/SASStoredProcess/do`

5.1.1 Taking Action on the URL

You can add parameters to the link to control the results display. The _action parameter allows you to control the view and functionality. If you add _action=TREE to the URL, the Web browser displays the list of stored processes.

From this view, when you run a stored process, the output displays in a separate Web browser tab with the full path. This is a quick way for developers to generate the URL when creating links for reports.

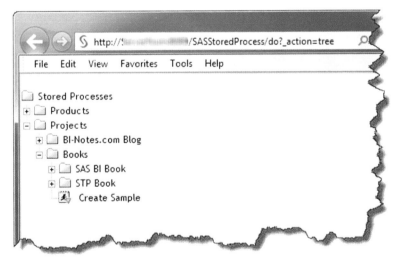

Figure 5-1 Using the _action=tree parameter

#19   Use _action=tree view to right-click and copy the full URL paths to stored processes. Edit this URL when creating chained stored processes or linking from BI reports and applications.

For example, after selecting the Create Sample stored process, the result appears in a new tab called SAS Output, and the _PROGRAM parameter contains the path and name of the stored process.

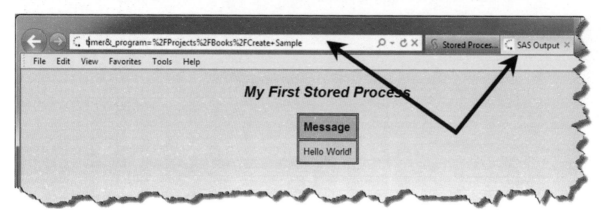

Figure 5-2 _Program parameter contains the path

The Create Sample stored process did not have any prompts. For stored process that use prompts and do not have a set default value, you might get a different result. For example, if you open the Date Prompt Report stored process (created in Section 2.3, "Using Date Prompts") an error message appears. The stored process bypassed the prompt window and produced an error.

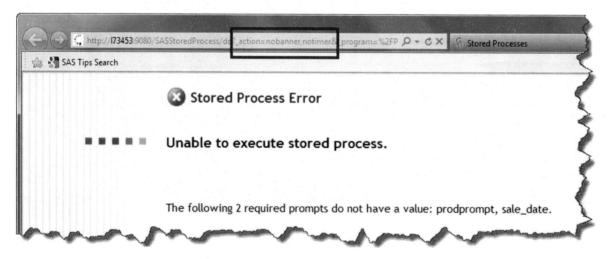

Figure 5-3 Error generates without prompt values

To display the prompt window, replace the _action=NOBANNER,NOTIMER to _action=PROPERTIES and press Enter. Use this URL if you need to refer to the stored process; it contains the parameters and full program path.

Figure 5-4 Using _action=properties parameter

Another common _action value is BACKGROUND. In a Chapter 11, "Generating Custom Output" we create a stored process that generates an email address but since the stored process sends the output as an email message no results are returned to the Web user. Because there is nothing for the user to see, this stored process is a good candidate for the _action=BACKGROUND parameter, which allows processes to run in the background.

 #20 The _action=BACKGROUND parameter runs your stored process without maintaining the link to your Web connection. See Chapter 9, "Improving Stored Process Performance" for more information.

When you select a stored process from the list to run in the background, the following message appears:

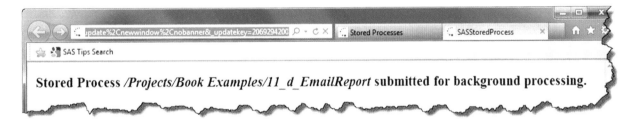

Figure 5-5 Using _action=background parameter

The _action parameter has some additional values that are useful. You can use multiple values by placing a comma between them.

Value	Description
NEWWINDOW	Displays the results in a new Web browser window.
NOBANNER	Removes the stored process banner from the top of the window. To continue displaying the prompts include both NOBANNER and PROPERTIES values separated by a comma.
DATA	Provides metadata information on where the stored process .sas program is stored, the execution server, and the result time.

#21 The _action values INDEX and DATA must be in upper case while all other options are not case sensitive. Use a comma to separate multiple values, such as: _action=DATA,XML

5.2 Debugging with the URL

When the stored process fails, a standard error message appears with a button to open the SAS log.

Figure 5-6 Standard Stored Process Error

If stored process results are not returned or are not as expected, review the log to determine what happened. Rather than asking the SAS administrator to get the most recent log off the server, you can add a parameter to the URL path to see the log quickly.

From the SAS Stored Process Web Application, add the **&_DEBUG=131** option to the URL path. For instance, when developing the program for Section 9.4, "Smart Messaging" the first window is blank. There is no error log because the program ran successfully.

In the URL bar, add **&_DEBUG=131** to the end of the path and press Enter.

Figure 5-7 Debug option added to URL

The log appears in the Web browser, similar to the log shown in Figure 5-8 "SAS Log". You can scroll or search the log to locate errors or read the log messages.

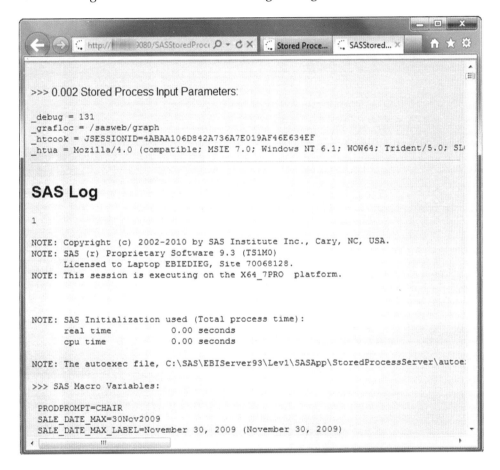

Figure 5-8 SAS Log

When creating custom forms and chaining stored process forms, the subsequent forms might not work using this method. During the development process, you must add the debug option as a hidden value. See Section 9.1, "Using Background Processing" for more information about adding hidden prompts.

#22 Use the &_debug=131 option in your custom HTML forms by adding this code string: <INPUT TYPE="HIDDEN" NAME="_debug" VALUE="131">

These methods only address streaming output to the Web browser. To view logs from stored processes that create a package of results only, you must include the _DEBUG_FILE option. This is especially useful when you are publishing package results to other web sites.

#23 Use the &_debug_file option to write debugging information for stored processes results into a location for retrieval.

5.3 Assigning the Log Locations

Stored process servers generate log messaging. If you have access to those locations, they can be an excellent place when troubleshooting programs. By default, the SAS Stored Process Server logs are maintained in the configuration directory of the SAS installation in the following subdirectory:

```
Lev1\SASApp\StoredProcessServer\Logs
```

#24 Put the stored process logs in a central location where they are easily accessible by the SAS Stored Process developers but away from the configuration files.

Many SAS administrators change the default stored process log location to create a central location for all log files and monitoring events. Another reason is to enable and manage developer access, while safeguarding the configuration files.

To change the default location, modify the LOGCONFIG.XML configuration file at:

```
<param name="FileNamePattern"
value=
"<config
dir>\Lev1\SASApp\StoredProcessServer\Logs\SASApp_STPServer_%d_%S{hostname}_%S{pid}.log"/>
```

5.4 Coding Options

Using macros for conditional logic, as shown in Section 9.4, "Smart Messaging" the log messages do not identify which conditions were found to be true or false. Developers frequently include the MLOGIC and MPRINT SAS macro options.

When you use the ODS automatic macros for %STPBEGIN and %STPEND, logging increases to include all of the content contained within these statements. You should include the MPRINT and MLOGIC options after the %STPBEGIN, and turn the options off before the %STPEND by using NOMPRINT and NOMLOGIC options.

To update Example 11-1, use the following example as a guideline.

Example 5-A Enabling Macro Logging	Required Modifications
	None of the marco code changes – omitting the code for brevity.
| ```
proc print data=work.qresult label
noobs;
run;
``` | |
| ```
%STPBEGIN;
  options mlogic mprint;
     %query;
  options nomlogic noprint;
%STPEND;
``` | Add the options around the QUERY macro so you only see the macro code associated with your code and not the macro coding the SAS system generates for the stored process. |

In Figure 5-9 "Using Macro Options", you can see the results of using the Marco options. In this case, the QRESULT table is not returning any values, which explains why there was no output.

```
41          +%STPBEGIN;
42          +options mlogic mprint;
43          +%query;
MLOGIC(QUERY): Beginning execution.
MPRINT(QUERY):   proc sql noprint;
MPRINT(QUERY):   create table qresult as select distinct state label="State", propcase(p
sum(actual) as actualsum label="Total Actual" format=dollar12., sum(predict)-sum(actual)
"30Nov2009"d and product = "CHAIR" group by state, product order by state ;
NOTE: Table WORK.QRESULT created, with 0 rows and 5 columns.

MLOGIC(QUERY): %IF condition &sqlobs > 0 is FALSE
MPRINT(QUERY):   select min(date) format=date9., max(date) format=date9. into :mindate,
NOTE: PROCEDURE SQL used (Total process time):
      real time          0.03 seconds
      cpu time           0.01 seconds


MPRINT(QUERY):   data qresult;
MPRINT(QUERY):   format Error $45.;
MPRINT(QUERY):   Error='Date Range Selected Returned 0 Values';
MPRINT(QUERY):  output;
MPRINT(QUERY):   Error="Current Data Between 01JAN2010 and 01DEC2011";
MPRINT(QUERY):  output;
```

Figure 5-9 Using Macro Options

 #25 You can add other SAS options, such as FULLSTIMER, to include timing information that can help you further understand the stored process performance.

5.5 Managing Folder Structures

When multiple groups are creating stored processes within an organization, it could lead to confusion if users use the same source code folder. Your organization might choose to set up multiple folders based on group or report type. For these source code folders, the SAS administrator must ensure that the proper permissions are in place.

#26 When multiple organizations have stored process developers, it is helpful to have different source code folders registered for each group of developers.

5.6 Accessing Data in Libraries

One of the most common issues when using stored processes is a user's ability to access the data table from the stored process. Typically, this situation arises because the user does not have permissions within the metadata or the physical folder structure is locked.

In the first situation, the user does not have access granted within the metadata. This is indicated by an error message similar to the following:

```
4          +libname candy meta library="Candy";
ERROR: No metadata objects found matching the specified URI.
ERROR: Error in the LIBNAME statement.
```

To correct this error, you (or the SAS administrator) must grant metadata authorization to the user.

In the second situation, if the issue is with access to the physical folder location, the error message is appears differently.

```
ERROR: User does not have appropriate authorization level for library CANDY.
ERROR: User does not have appropriate authorization level for library CANDY.
```

If the request runs on the standard SAS Workspace Server, the user who submitted the request must have access to the physical data location.

If the stored process is running on the SAS Stored Process server, the user ID running the service, typically SASSRV, requests the access to the physical files. However, when the stored process is running on the SAS Workplace Server, which executes on the pooled workspace server, the host uses SASSRV to access the physical files.

To resolve the permission issues, SAS Institute suggests using a *mediated-access* method, where the application service ID SASSRV has full access to the physical data, and the SAS Metadata Server grants access to the individual user. Another benefit to this method is that it reduces the need to set up user accounts on the host server environment.

5.6.1 Making 9.3 Stored Processes Compatible for 4.3 Clients

While navigating through the SAS folders from 4.3 version of SAS Enterprise Guide or SAS Add-in to Microsoft Office, the following notice highlights the fact that no compatible stored processes exist.

If you registered the stored process from the SAS Management Console in version 9.3, it will only open in 4.3 SAS clients when the stored process is made compatible with prior versions. The SAS administrator can make the stored process compatible with version 9.2 stored processes.

#27 You can make stored processes compatible with SAS Version 9.3 only when they were set to run on a specific logical server.

To make the stored process compatible, follow these steps:

1. From the SAS Management Console, navigate to the stored process you want to convert.

2. Open the stored process and ensure it is set to run on a specific logical server instead of the Default Server.

3. Right-click the stored process, select **Make Compatible** from the pop-up menu.

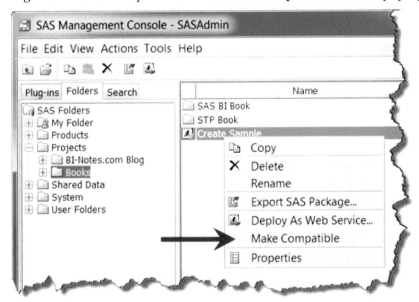

4. Test the stored process to ensure it works in the SAS 9.2 environment.

Using SAS Enterprise Guide

SAS Enterprise Guide is a Windows application that provides a point-and-click desktop interface to SAS programs. In this chapter, you will learn how to use SAS Enterprise Guide to create, run, and modify stored processes. SAS Enterprise Guide is an all-in-one tool for stored processes. Many developers prefer to use SAS Enterprise Guide because they have easier access to the libraries, project prompts, and code wizards.

6.1 Registering a Stored Process

In Chapter 2, "Creating Simple Stored Processes" you learned how to use the SAS Management Console and SAS Enterprise Guide 5.1 to create a stored process. SAS Enterprise Guide allows you to register stored processes, but it also allows you to develop and test within the same application. The SAS Stored Process Wizard provides a step-by-step guide to creating a stored process. If you are using SAS Enterprise Guide versions 4.3 and prior, use the following process to register a stored process.

1. From SAS Enterprise Guide, select the Stored Process wizard using one of these methods:

    -   From the File menu❶, select **New > Stored Process**.

    -   From the Project Tree❷, right-click the task or program and select **Create Stored Process**.

    -   From the Process Flow open area❸, right-click and select **Create Stored Process**.

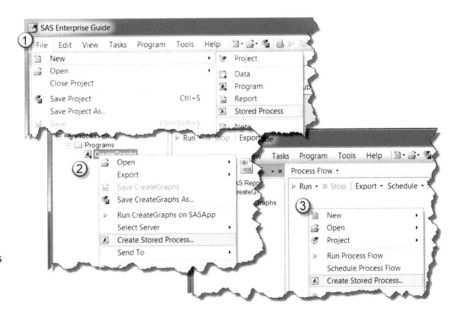

2. The SAS Stored Process Wizard appears. In the Create New SAS Stored Process Wizard window, you start the first of seven steps. The first step is to name and describe the stored process.

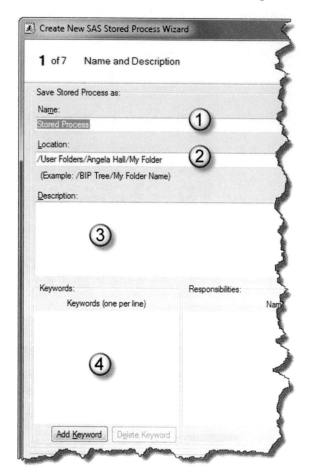

	Field	Description
1	Name	Text used by the metadata. This text is what the end-user sees.
2	Location	Use the Browse button to navigate to the location where you want to save the stored process on the metadata folder.
3	Description	As you create more stored processes, it is useful to provide additional details that can assist locating the stored process, remembering the requestor, and determining who is responsible for maintaining it.
4	Keywords	Add keywords to help users search for the stored process from SAS Information Delivery Portal or other SAS BI clients.

3. From step 2, edit the code and options as needed. If you are basing the stored process on an existing program or process flow, the wizard imports the code automatically. Then, you can make edits to the program.

    Note: Use **Replace with code** to import a program from the project or from another directory.

When you make changes to the program, the wizard reminds you before saving the stored process that it does match your original code and offers to copy the code. Likewise, if you change the program outside of the stored process, when you modify the stored process, it allows you to choose the version you want to use.

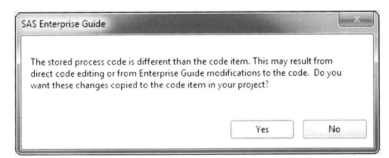

Because SAS Enterprise Guide automatically includes %STPBEGIN and %STPEND macros, if you do not want those macros included, select **Include code for** and select the **Stored process macros** option to deselect it.

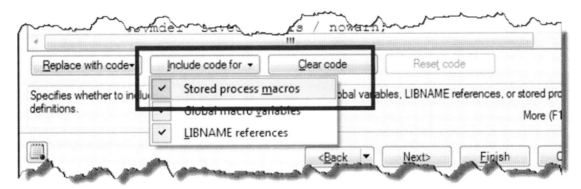

#28 **The SAS Enterprise Guide Stored Process Wizard inserts the %STPBEGIN and %STPEND macros into the stored process by default. You can turn them off by clearing the box in the Include code for menu.**

4. The third step provides the ability to select the execution server, provide the source, and select the result type. See Section 1.2, "Registering a SAS Stored Process" for a more complete description of each item.

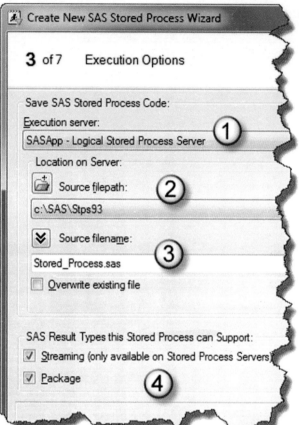

	Field	Description
1	Execution server	Select the server that executes the stored process.
2	Source filepath	Select the SAS code stored path. This is the physical program location. Select Folder to navigate to the source code repository your SAS administrator has made available for storing code.
3	Source filename	Type a program name. SAS code is stored in a source code repository (listed in the Source filepath field). When you save the SAS code, use the .sas file extension.
4	SAS Result Types	Select the result type that you want. In SAS Enterprise Guide 4.3, the result type note concerning streaming output is available on Stored Process Servers only and does not apply to the SAS 9.3 system. See Section 1.2, "Registering a SAS Stored Process" for more information about server types and result capabilities.

5. In the fourth step, the SAS system automatically lists the libraries in the code. If you want this library reference included in the code, select the LIBREF checkbox. You can also add another library by checking the Use custom LIBNAME statement checkbox and typing the LIBREF in the field.

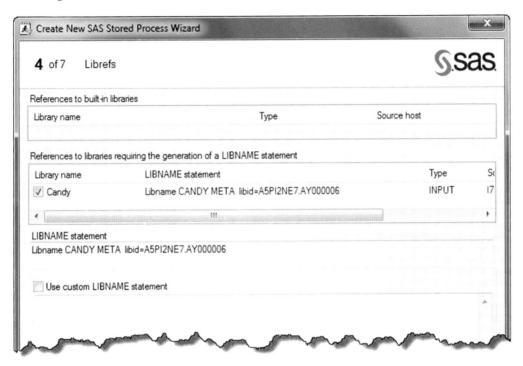

6. In the next window, you can assign the prompts to your stored process.

    You can add as many prompts as you need. For this example, you must have a prompt for every macro variable in the WHERE statement. Otherwise, the stored process generates an error and does not run. There are three methods for using prompts with the stored processes: using a project prompt, creating a prompt, and using a shared prompt. You can use one or more of these methods within the stored process.

    When converting a task or the entire project with a prompt, the wizard imports the prompts automatically. You can define new prompts using the **New ❶** drop-down menu. To include output parameters, use the **Output Parameters ❷** button. (See Section 7.1, "Working with SAS Information Map Studio" for an example of output parameters usage.)

7. Define input data sources and output data targets in Step 6. See Section 7.3, "Using the SAS Add-in for Microsoft Office" for an example about how to use this option.

8. In the last window, you can review the stored process to ensure that everything is set up correctly. Select **Finish** to register and run the stored process.

6.2 Running Stored Processes

In Section 1.1.1, "Accessing a Stored Process from the Web" you learned how to run a stored process from the Web browser. SAS Enterprise Guide allows you to open and run a stored process or run a stored process that you already created and have associated with the project.

6.2.1 Adding a Stored Process to your Project

To add a stored process, follow these steps:

1. Select **File > Open > Stored Process**. In the Open Stored Process window, navigate to the folder that contains the stored process and double-click it. The stored process appears in your Project Tree.

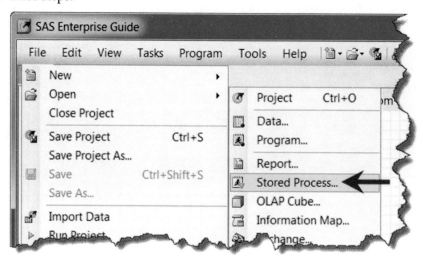

2. After you have added your project, select the stored process and select Run.

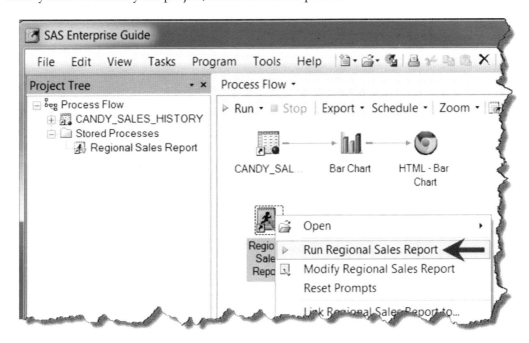

6.3 Modifying Stored Processes

After opening or creating a stored process, you can modify the properties or code by right-clicking on the stored process and choosing **Modify <*stored process name*>**, where <*stored process name*> is the name of your stored process.

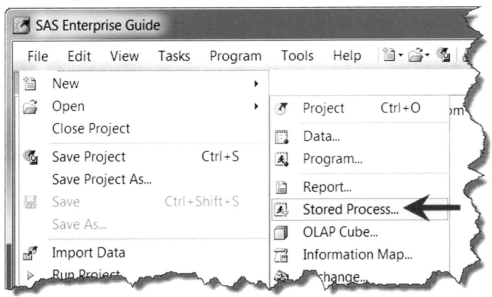

Figure 6-1 Modifying a Stored Process from SAS Enterprise Guide

#29   Edit the stored process code through SAS Enterprise Guide by selecting File> Open >Stored Process and navigate to the metadata folder where stored processes are registered.

You can modify any of the selections that you made while creating your stored processes. Select **SAS Code** from the left menu to make changes to the code itself.

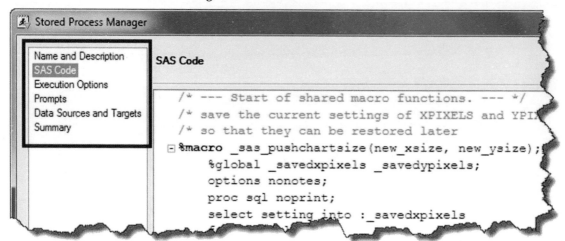

Figure 6-2 Using the Stored Process Manager

Many developers find it easier to make changes in SAS Enterprise Guide so they have a local copy of the code. When the code associated with the stored process changes, the stored process wizard prompts you to select which code you want to use going forward. Select **Use EG Code** to use the changes made in the SAS Enterprise Guide project, shown in Figure 6-3.

If you changed the stored process code without using SAS Enterprise Guide, you might have used a code editor. If this is the case, you can subsequently use SAS Enterprise Guide code to update your local copy. Select **Use Server Code** to keep the code on the server and replace your local copy.

 #30 Syncing code from SAS Enterprise Guide to the stored process allows you to use the editing and testing features making it a better coding interface. To maintain active links between the initial code and the stored process, save the SAS Enterprise Guide project and use it in the future when making changes.

Figure 6-3 Comparing SAS files

Using SAS BI Clients

One of the major benefits of using stored processes is extendibility. SAS stored processes are one of the most customizable products; there are several advantages, such as the ability to set up reports that can run in various locations, enhance out-of-the box functionality with custom widgets, and leverage all of the stored process server options. In this chapter, you will learn tips and tricks for using stored processes within SAS BI clients.

7.1 Working with the SAS Information Map Studio

SAS Stored Processes provide additional functionality for information maps, such as adding prompts and pre-joining data tables where some tricky SQL joins might be required. Typically, information maps are the primary data source for SAS Web Report Studio.

7.1.1 Dynamically determine datasets

You can leverage stored processes to determine which data tables to join based on what the user selects within a prompt. When you have several data tables, you can speed up the processing time by joining the needed datasets only. In the following example, you will work with the Candy Company to better use their immense amounts of data while keeping the information maps speedy!

The Candy Company has all of their detailed sales data stored in datasets arranged by year. In this example, the Candy Company has five large datasets, one for each of the past five years. All of the 2011 records are in a dataset named SALESDETAIL2011 and all of the 2010 records are in a dataset named SALESDETAIL2010, and so on. Rather than attempt to join all data or create multiple information maps and reports, we can use the date range that our user selects to determine which data table to include.

 #31 **If your stored process is not in the SAS Information Map Studio list, it was set to run on the SAS Stored Process Server only. Update the metadata to allow your stored process to run on both the Stored Process Server and the SAS Workspace Server.**

In order for this stored process to work, you must maintain a table definition within the metadata for the information map to use. Follow these steps to complete this task.

1. Create a metadata library and define a table within the metadata.

To avoid manually adding the metadata, create a blank table and use the register table wizard in SAS Management Console (or SAS Enterprise Guide Update Library tool). Later, you can delete the table from the physical folder location.

a. Create the temporary folder c:\sas\data\tempout.

b. From SAS Enterprise Guide or BASE SAS, run the following code to create a sample dataset. The WHERE statement must generate an empty table. This is useful for systems with limited data space because only the metadata is needed for subsequent steps.

```
libname tempout "c:\sas\data\tempout";
data tempout.salesdetail;
  set booksamp.salesdetail2011(where=(date="01oct74"d));
run;
```

c. Register a BASE SAS library called TempOut that points to the c:\sas\data\tempout folder.

d. Register the SalesDetail dataset.

e. Delete SalesDetail.sas7bdat from the c:\sas\data\tempout folder. The stored process recreates this data, and you only need to register it in the metadata. When the stored process runs, it places the resulting dataset in a WORK version of the metadata library and table you created in step 1.

2. Create a stored process that reviews the date range and includes the desired data records.

Example 7-A IMAP Dynamic Table	Notes

`%stpbegin;`
 	
`libname tempout (work);`
	Create a library reference called tempout that points to the same location as the temporary WORK file folder.

	You must use the exact LIBREF name as the metadata library that you created in step 1.

`libname booksamp meta`
`  library="STP Book Sample Data"`
`  metaout=data;`
	Assign the metadata library.

`data _null_;`
 	
`year1=substr("&date_range_min", 6, 4);`
`year2=substr("&date_range_max", 6, 4);`
	Create two temporary macros (Start and End) that only contain the 4-digit year (for example, 2012). When the stored process runs, these macro variables come from a date_range prompt.

`call symput('start', year1);` `call symput('end', year2);`	Create a macro for the current year to reduce the maintenance of the do loop in the next step.

`year3=year(today());`
`call symput('current', strip(year3));`
 	
`run;`	

`%macro join;` `data &_TARGET_newdat;`	Set the name of the output dataset, which is the &_TARGET_newdat macro variable.
	Note: NEWDAT is the name of the hidden prompt, which contains the full LIBREF dataset name.

Example 7-A IMAP Dynamic Table	Notes
```set %do i=2008 %to &current; %if &i >= &start and &i <= &end %then booksamp.salesdetail&i ; %end; ;```	Loop through all years available (in this case 2008 to the current year) and set the necessary data sets.
```run; %mend; %join; %stpend;```	Stop the data step, end the join macro, run the JOIN macro and close the stored process.

3. Register this stored process by following these steps.

   a. In the Execution tab, ensure that the Result capabilities: checkboxes are not checked. Refer to Section 1.2.5, "Understanding the Result Capabilities" for more details about results.

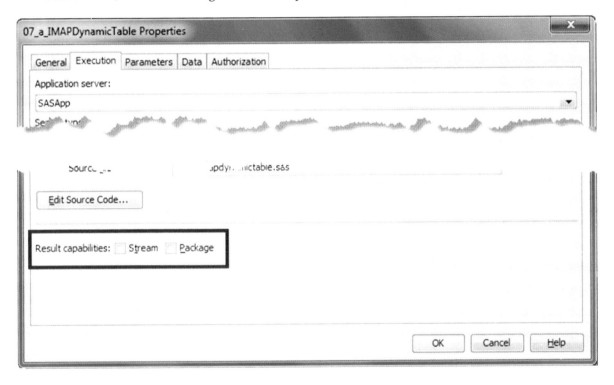

b. Add a date range prompt for the DATE_RANGE macro referenced in the stored process code.

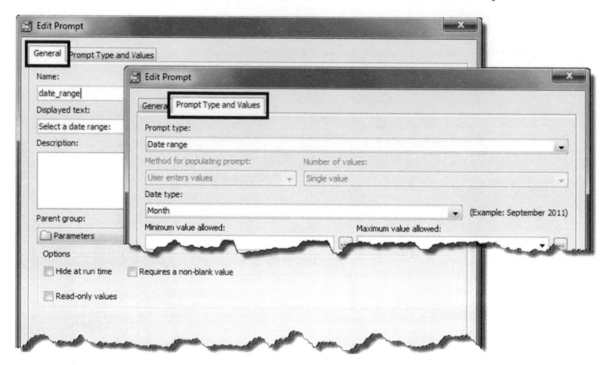

c. Add a data source prompt called newdat, which has the default value of TEMPOUT.SALESDETAIL dataset. Note that this is the library and dataset name used in step 1.

To prevent the user from seeing this prompt, check the **Hide at run time** checkbox.

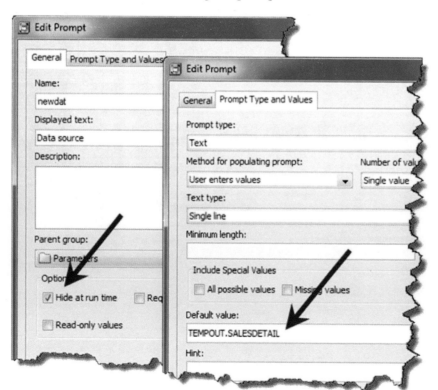

d. In the Data tab, add **newdat** as the target dataset in the New Data Target area. This newdat prompt is then responsible for converting &_TARGET_newdat into TEMPOUT.SALESDETAIL.

e. In the New Data Target area, click **Select** and choose the **TEMPOUT.SALESDETAIL** table from the corresponding metadata folder.

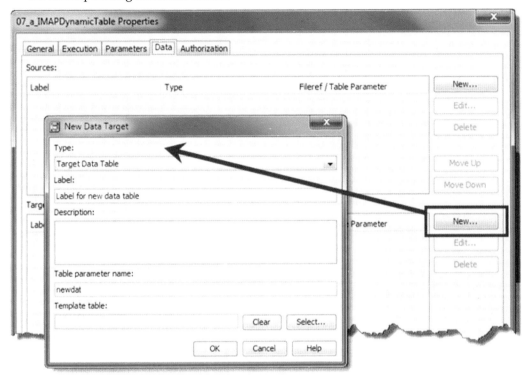

4. In SAS Information Map Studio, create a new information map using the metadata table that you defined in step 1.

5. After a table is created in the information map, you can add the stored process.

   a. Select **Stored processes** ❶ from the Show menu.

   b. Navigate to the table location in TEMPout library❷.

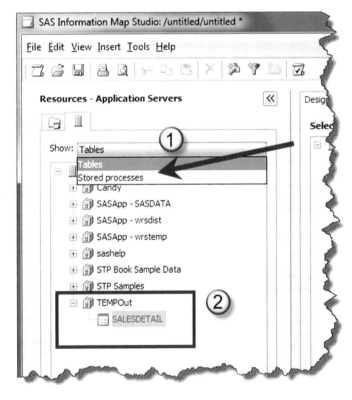

6. When testing the information map, use **View SQL and Show Server Log** to review the code.

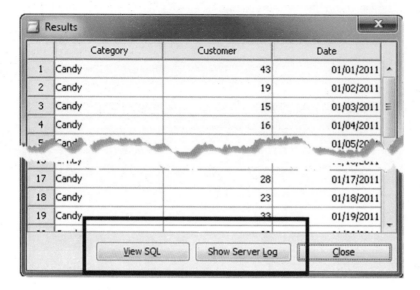

Using the log as a guide, walk through the sequence to understand the results more clearly.

Log from Example 7-A	Notes

2 LIBNAME tempout BASE "C:\SAS\Data\TempOut";
NOTE: Libref TEMPOUT was successfully assigned as follows:
    Engine: BASE
    Physical Name: C:\SAS\Data\TempOut
	SAS Information Map Studio automatically assigns the metadata library TEMPOUT based on the metadata. Later, this library is reassigned to point to the temporary WORK location.

4 /* v2 (9.3) stored process support */ 5 PROC STP program='/Projects/Books/STP Book/07_a_IMAPDynamicTable(StoredProcess)'; 6 outputData NewDat=TEMPOUT.SALESDETAIL; 7 inputParam NewDat='TEMPOUT.SALESDETAIL'; 8 inputParam date_range='February 2011 September 2011'; 9 run; NOTE: PROC_STP: ====== Proc STP Execution Starting ====== NOTE: PROC_STP: ====== Stored Process: /Projects/Books/STP Book/07_a_IMAPDynamicTable(StoredProcess) ======	SAS uses the PROC STP procedure to execute stored processes. The NewDat prompt equals the default value TEMPOUT.SALESDETAIL.
NOTE: %INCLUDE (level 1) file c:\SAS\Stps93\07_a_imapdynamictable.sas is file c:\SAS\Stps93\07_a_imapdynamictable.sas.	SAS includes the physical SAS code for the stored process.

2 +%stpbegin;
3 +libname tempout (work);
NOTE: Libref TEMPOUT was successfully assigned as follows:
 	
    Levels: 1
    Engine(1):   V9
	Calls the stored process macro and reassigns the LIBREF tempout to the temporary WORK folder, which was created when the session started.

Log from Example 7-A	Notes
``` Physical Name(1): C:\Users\sassrv\AppData\Local\Temp\SAS Temporary Files_TD8804_L73453_\Prc3 ```	
	The stored process code runs.
``` NOTE: The data set SP_TEMPO.SALESDETAIL has 2901 observations and 17 variables. ```	The stored process created the SP_TEMPO.SALESDETAIL dataset and returned the dataset to the information map. The information map sees as the TempOut.SalesDetail target data.

7.1.2 Adding Prompts to an Information Map

The Candy Company wants to use a cascading prompt group for Fiscal Year and Fiscal Quarter inside an information map. When users select the information map, they select the desired year and quarter. This means that the developer does not need to create a separate information map for each year and quarter, which prevents a potential administration nightmare.

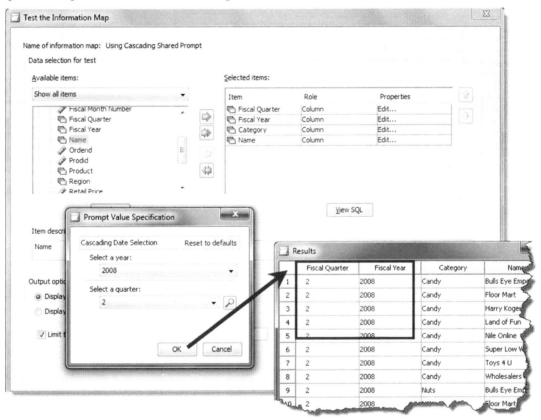

Figure 7-1 Using cascading prompts with an Information Map

When attempting to add the prompt group, the shared cascading prompt does not appear. In SAS Information Map Studio, you cannot create all prompt types. In these cases, you can use the stored process to define the prompt and code the data elements in the information map to use these parameters.

#32   Stored processes can contain more prompt options than information maps. Attach a stored process to an information map and use code within the information map to leverage these additional prompts.

Create a Prompt Group

Follow these steps to create the stored process and modify the information map to use the stored process.

1.   Register a new stored process.

   a.   This stored process does not contain any code. It simply runs the prompts and produces the result. In the Execution tab, select the Source Code Repository and point to an empty .sas file.

   b.   In the Parameters tab, select **Add Shared**. Then, navigate to the area where your organization would store shared prompts and add the shared prompt group. See Section 4.1.1, "Setting the Stored Process Style" for more details about shared prompts.

   c.   In the New Output Parameter area, select **New** and create two new string output parameters, one for Year ❶ and one for Quarter ❷.

      After the stored process runs, you want it to forward the values from the Year and Quarter prompts to the information map. The output parameters contain the values sent to the map.

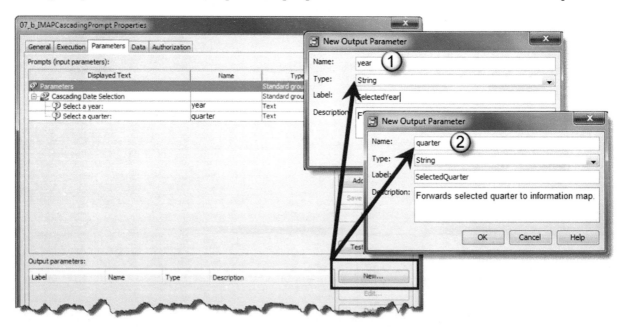

Within SAS Information Map Studio, add the new stored process to your existing map. Change the Show drop-down❶ to **Stored processes**. Select the stored process❷ you want to include. The stored process appears in the Selected Resources area❸.

2. Add a custom filter that references the Quarter and Year prompts from the stored process. Use the prompt macro variable in the expression.

   Note: In the Filter combinations field, note that Fiscal_Year and Fiscal_Quarter are combined.

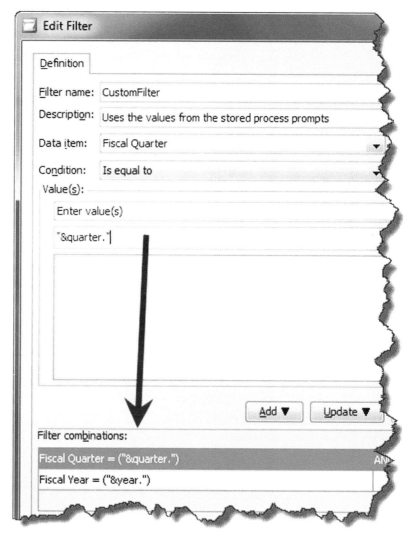

#33 As an alternative to creating filters, you can use the custom expression window in a new data element to leverage stored process prompts.

3. Add the filter as a general pre-filter, so that every time the user accesses the information map, the prompt values are available to the resulting query.

    a. Select the information map name and select **Properties ❶** from the pop-up menu.

    b. Move the **Available filters** to the **Selected filters** area with the related table**❷**.

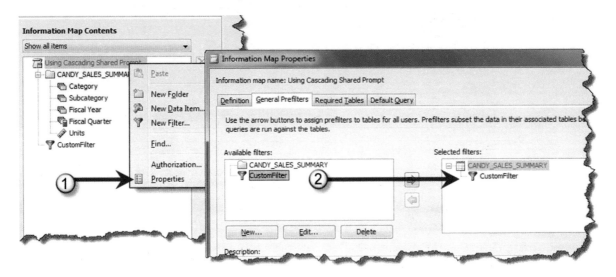

4. Test your information map. The result should be similar to Figure 7-1.

7.2 Using SAS Web Report Studio

Use SAS Web Report Studio to add a stored process to display a table or chart within a Web Report Studio report. You can integrate a stored process with existing reports to make use of the prompts because you can use a prompt to work with the group breaks. For the following examples, let's use the Furniture Company sales reports created in Section 2.2, "Creating a Stored Process with a Single Prompt".

7.2.1 Display Stored Process Reports

In this example, the Furniture Company wants to open the sales report in SAS Web Report Studio. The sales analysts want the Web Report Studio reports to feature some of the sales reports already available.

Follow these steps to add a stored process to the report.

1. From SAS Management Console, open the stored process that creates the sales report. Ensure that the stored process can output to Package by selecting the **Package** checkbox.

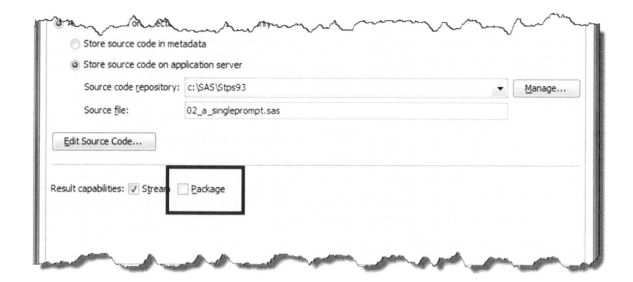

2. In SAS Web Report Studio, create a new report. Select the Stored Process icon from the tool bar and drag to the report area.

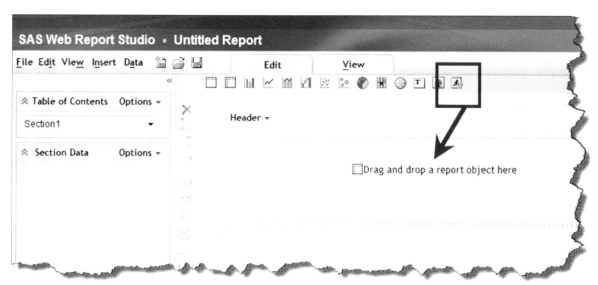

3. Right-click the stored process box and select **Edit**. In the **Insert Stored Process** window, select the Sales Report stored process to add it to the report.

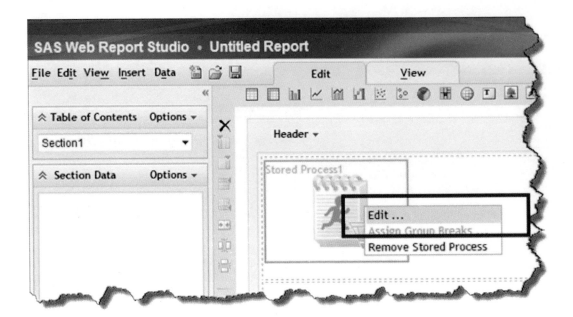

4. Select the View tab, to see the report. The report prompts you for the product and then displays the results.

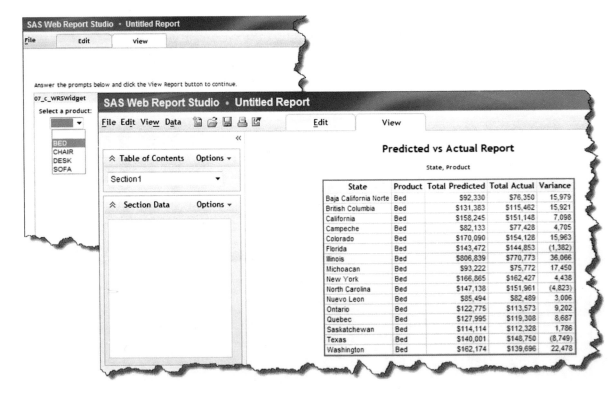

The 50 Keys To Learning SAS® Stored Processes

7.2.2 Linking Group Breaks to Stored Processes

The Furniture Company prefers that the prompt for the stored process exist on the left panel rather than having the user see the prompt screen before the result. In the following example, you will edit the Web report (created in Section 7.2.1) to use group breaks.

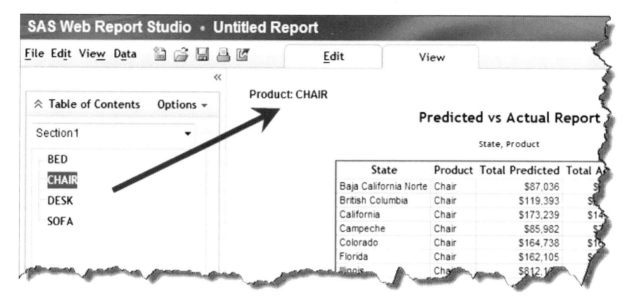

Figure 7-2 Linking Groups

To enable group breaks, the data set or information must be available. After the data is available, the group breaks option becomes available. Because the previous report included the stored process only, there was no reason to add the data.

Follow these steps to add group breaks to the report.

1. On the Edit tab, select **Data>Select Data**. Add the dataset that contains the product list.

2. In the Section pane, select **Options>Group Breaks**.

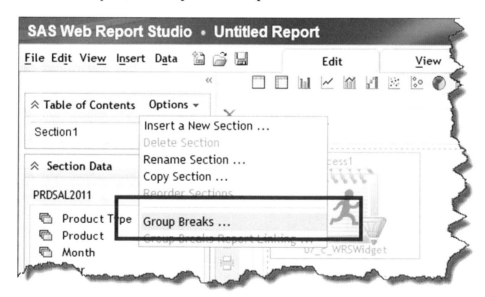

3. From the **Break by values of** drop-down list, select **Product**.

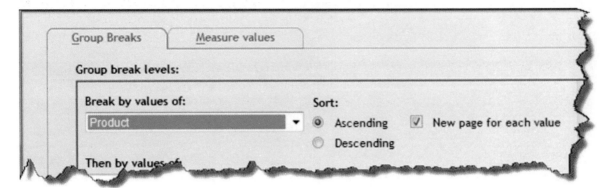

4. Right-click on the stored process widget and select **Assign Group Breaks**.

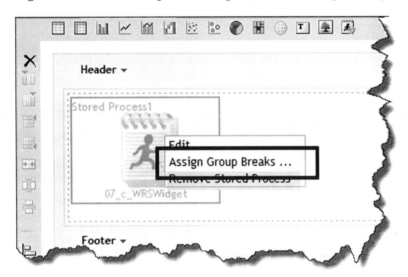

5. In the Select a product drop-down list, select **Product**.

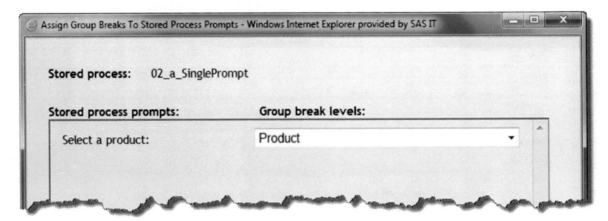

6. Save these changes and view the report to see the results shown previously in Figure 7-2.

7.2.3 Drilling into Data with a Stored Process

Previously, the Furniture Company was using the SAS Stored Process Web Application to run one report and link to another report. After using SAS Web Report Studio, the analysts ask that the report developers create a Web reports that navigate to the detailed report as needed.

In Section 3.3, "Chaining Reports" you learned how to chain stored processes by placing the URL in the stored process code. The following example places the URL in the information map instead so report developers have the variable available for new web reports. End users of the web report can select the link to view the detailed stored process report.

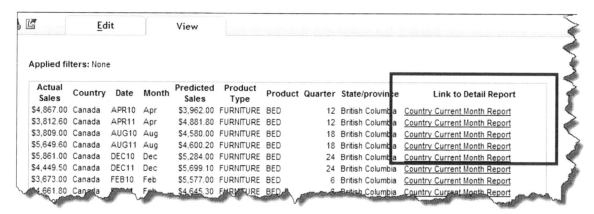

Figure 7-3 Using a URL link with a report

Follow these steps to add a HTML link to your stored process report.

1. From SAS Information Map Studio, create an information map for the PRDSALE2011 dataset. Create a new data item by selecting the **New Data Item** icon on the menu bar.

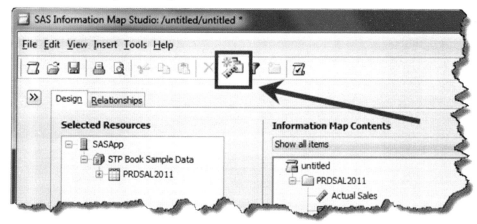

2. From the Data Item Properties window, name the data item **Link to Detail Report** and select the **Edit** button to add the URL code using the Expression Editor.

3. Copy the URL path from the example in Section 3.3.2, "Updating the Summary Report with a URL" and paste it within the Expression Text field:

"<a href='http://&_srvname:&_srvport/SASStoredProcess/do?%NRSTR(&_program)=&_metafolder.Sales+Detail%NRSTR(&sale_date_min)=&sale_date_min

%NRSTR(&sale_date_max)=&sale_date_max"||"%NRSTR(&prodprompt)="

||STRIP(product)||"NRSTR(&state)="||STRIP(state)||"'>Detailed Report</a>"

4. Because the stored process is running outside of the stored process web application, the **&_srvname, &_srvport** and **&_metafolder** reserved macro values must be modified to reflect the actual machine name, port number, and stored process location.

5. Add the associated data items to complete the URL expression. There are two STRIP() functions, one for State and one for Product. Also there are two sales date prompts called &sale_date_max and &sale_date_min, these will need to use the same date field from the table.

   a. From the Data Sources tab, select the data item you want to add.

   b. Place the cursor inside the first STRIP() function and select **Add to Expression** to move the data item to the STRIP() function.

   c. Modify the &sale_date_min and &sale_date_max to put(<<root.DATE>>, date7.)

   d. Repeat this step for any other data items you want to add.

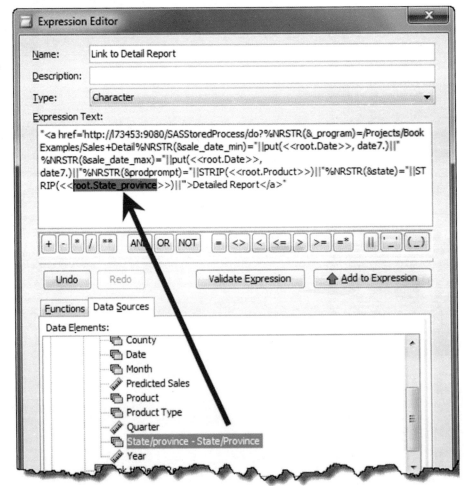

6. Return to the Data Item Properties window, select **Classifications, Aggregations, and Format.** In the Formats area, select the **Display as Hyperlink** checkbox.

7. From SAS Web Report Studio, add this information map and create a table. The results should resemble Figure 7-3.

 #34 Use the Display as Hyperlink checkbox in the information map so SAS Web Report Studio interprets the HTML code correctly.

7.3 Using the SAS Add-in for Microsoft Office

Users with the SAS Add-in for Microsoft Office component can quickly run stored processes and interact with stored processes from Word, Excel, PowerPoint, and Outlook.

7.3.1 Running a Stored Process

The SAS Add-in for Microsoft Office adds a SAS ribbon to Excel, Word, and PowerPoint. After selecting the SAS menu, choose the Reports icon to select an existing stored process.

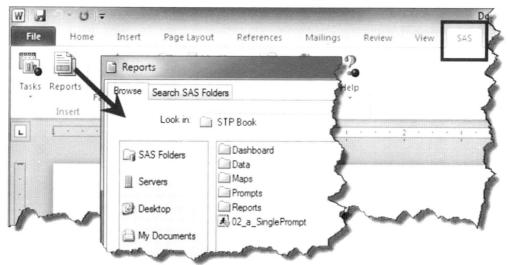

Figure 7-4 Opening a SAS Stored Process in Microsoft Office

In Outlook, use the **SAS Central** icon from the SAS ribbon. SAS Central appears in the list that you can navigate to find the desired stored process. After running the report, you can save or share the stored process.

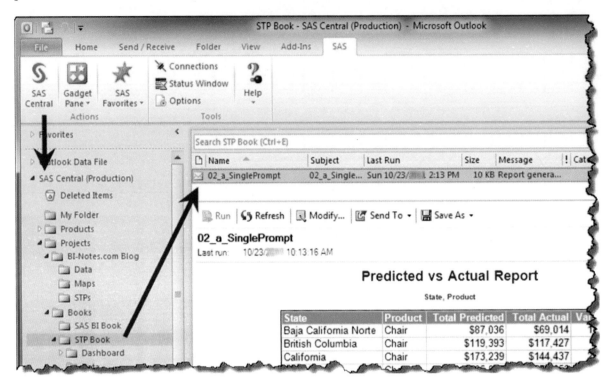

Figure 7-5 Opening a Stored Process in Microsoft Outlook

7.3.2 Using Data Sources and Targets

Instead of using a SAS dataset as the source for a stored process, you can create a stored process that allows a user to select data from a spreadsheet and run the stored process based on that data. The Candy Company wants to generate a Pareto chart of data in their Microsoft Excel spreadsheet, but they do not have the license for the SAS Quality Control component to use the SAS Add-in to Microsoft Office task.

This is how this process would work:

1. The sales analyst uses the **SAS Data** icon to open the BOOKSAMP.SALESDETAIL2011. She is interested in a Pareto chart of total sales for the products. She can edit the data or remove any un-needed columns.

2. She selects the rows that she wants to analyze and two columns: Product and Sale_Amount.

3. Select the **SAS Reports** icon, navigate to the stored process, and double-click the name to run it.

4. The stored process prompts her for the column names from the selected area.

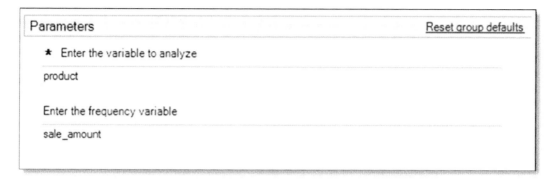

5. The next window appears allowing her to supply the input data source and the output worksheet. Because the analyst selected the spreadsheet range A1:B501 before running the stored process, the stored process captures the value for the first prompt.

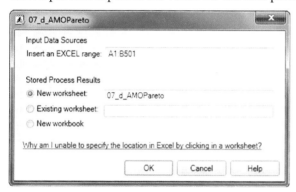

6. The Pareto chart analysis appears in the indicated worksheet.

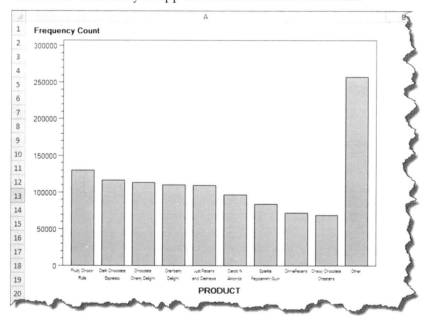

To accomplish this task, you must create a new stored process and use some new stored process options when you register the stored process.

7.4 Creating the Stored Process

This stored process leverages the XML LIBNAME engine. Refer to the SAS XML LIBNAME Engine User Guide Documentation for more information on how that works.

Example 7-C AMO Pareto	Notes
```%stpbegin;``` ```libname NEWDAT xml;```	Start the stored process macro. Open an XML library called NEWDAT. This corresponds to the FILEREF field in the Stored Process Source Data definition.

```proc freq noprint```
``` data=NEWDAT.&_WEBIN_SASNAME ;```
```tables &var1```
```   / out=temp norow nocol;```
```weight &var2;```
```run;```
	The NEWDAT library points to the XML library created above. &_WEBIN_SASNAME is a reserved macro variable, which represents the incoming data stream.
	
	VAR1 holds the Product column, and VAR2 is the Sale_Amount column in this example.

```proc sort data=work.temp;```
```by descending percent;```
```run;```
```data temp2(drop=newcount);```
```set temp end=last;```
```total+percent;```
```if total <=80 then output;```
```if total > 80 then do;```
``` &var1='Other';```
``` newcount+count;```
```end;```
```if last then do;```
``` count=newcount;```
``` output;```
```end;```
```run;```
	Use PROC SORT and a data step to sort the data in descending order and reorganize the data into the 80/20 Pareto distribution display.

```proc sql noprint;```
``` select &VAR1```
```   into :VALS separated```
```   by '" "' from work.temp2;```
``` quit;```
```axis1 order=("&VALS");```
	All the variables sent to the &VALS macro variable from the analysis table and are included in the AXIS statement.
	
	This maintains the descending order for the top 80% with the Other category containing everything else.

```proc gchart data=work.temp2;```
``` vbar &VAR1```
```   /sumvar=count maxis=axis1;```
```run; quit;```
	Print the graph.

```%stpend;```	Close the stored process macro.

7.4.1 Registering the Stored Process

When you register this stored process code, you will need to use a couple of tricks.

1. In SAS Management Console, register the stored process.

    Hint: The stored process must be made compatible to work with SAS Add-in to MS Office 4.3.

2. In the Execution tab, choose the **Stored Process Server**. (The input and output data streams are not available in the Workspace Server.)

3. Create the two text prompts for the user to type the columns names used by the stored process. **VAR1** corresponds to the prompt text "Enter a variable to analyze" and **VAR2** corresponds to the "Enter the frequency variable" selection. These prompts are required for this example to return results.

4. From the Data tab, select **New** for the Sources area.

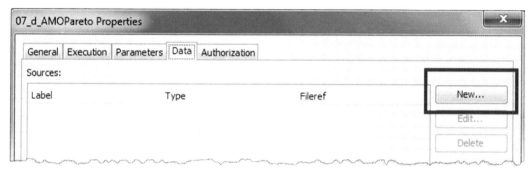

5. Define the incoming data source as an XML Stream using these steps:

    a. From the Type drop-down, select **XML Stream**.

        Hint: If the type drop-down box states **XML Data Source** the stored process is only compatible with SAS Add-in to MS Office 5.1.

    b. In the Label field, type **Insert an EXCEL range.** This ensures that the user understands that a data range is required.

    c. In the Fileref field, type **newdata** (the name you used for the LIBREF).

    d. Select the **Allow rewinding stream** checkbox.

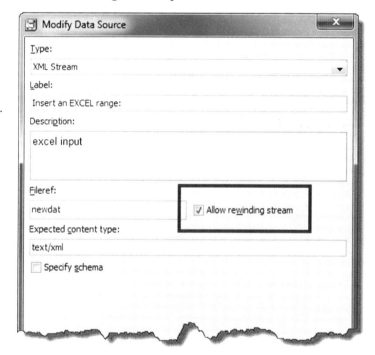

6. Save the stored process. Complete a test run to ensure that it works properly.

Using the SAS BI Web Clients

SAS Stored Processes provide more power to the SAS BI Web clients. In this chapter, you will learn ways to use the stored processes with the SAS BI Dashboard and the SAS Information Delivery Portal.

8.1 SAS Business Intelligence Dashboard

The SAS Business Intelligence (BI) Dashboard provides a point-and-click interface that lets you create quick summary reports with multiple and interactive report elements. You can add stored processes to extend the functionality of this versatile system even further. The SAS BI Dashboard contains a different set of prompting capabilities, which are combined and displayed on the same page as the result. Selections the users make from dashboard prompts are forwarded as parameters into stored processes.

8.1.1 Creating Data Sources for Users

In our next example, we will assume that the Candy Company has purchased the Furniture Company. The new general manager wants to see the sales figures for both companies as soon as possible.

The data exists in different systems; however, the Furniture Company must ensure that the data is available. Alternatively, the Candy Company needs to ensure that all of the regional quarterly sales data is available to dashboard designers.

You can use a stored process to provide a data source for the dashboard. This setup is often necessary when the dashboard needs to have data refreshed or queried dynamically based on user selections or when the dataset does not already

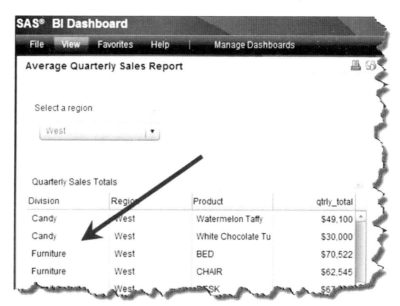

Figure 8-1 Dashboard containing two different data sources

exist within the metadata.

When creating a dashboard dataset, the stored process must use the SAS Publishing Framework to generate a package on the SAS Content Server. Each time a user needs the data source, the stored processes creates the dataset in a temporary location in the user's work directory. The dataset is available as long as the user remains connected.

Creating the Stored Process

As mentioned earlier the Candy and Furniture Companies combined. In the following example, these data systems (SALESDETAIL2011 and PRDSALE2011) are queried and combined each time the dashboard is viewed ensuring that executives are reviewing the most up to date information for both divisions.

Example 8-A BID Data Source	Notes
~~%stpbegin;~~	Do not include %STPBEGIN and %STPEND macros.
`%global region;`	Define the prompt as a global macro.
`libname booksamp meta` `    library="STP Book Sample Data";`	Assign the metadata library.

`proc sql;`
`  create table result1 as`
`  select distinct`
`    'Candy' as Division length=25`
`    ,region`
`    ,product`
`    ,sum(sale_amount) as Qtrly_total`
`  from booksamp.salesdetail2011`
`  where date >= intnx('quarter', today(), -1)`
`      and region= "&region"`
`group by product, region;`
 	
`create table result2 as`
`  select distinct`
`    'Furniture' as Division length=25`
`  ,case`
`    when country= 'U.S.A.'  then 'Central'`
`    when country= 'Mexico' then 'West'`
`                            else 'East'`
`    end as region`
`  ,product`
`  ,sum(actual) as Qtrly_total`
`from booksamp.prdsal2011`
`    where  date >= intnx('quarter', today(), -1)`
`      and calculated region= "&region"`
`group by product, region;`
	Generate the summarized data from each system and join into one dataset.
	
	Ensure that the regions from PRDSAL3 match those in the Candy Company datasets.

Example 8-A BID Data Source	Notes
```\nquit;\n\ndata RecentUnit;\nset result1 result2;\nrun;\n```	
```\n%let temploc = %sysfunc(pathname(work));\n```	Create a macro variable that contains the physical path of the user's session work location. This ensures that the data result package is unique to each user session and is removed when the session closes automatically.
```\ndata null;\nlength path $32767;\nrc = 0;\npid = 0 ;\ndescription = '0';\nname = '';\ncall package_begin(pid, description, name, rc);\n```	Begin the package-publishing step. This places the package in the SAS Publishing Framework.
```\ncall insert_dataset(pid, "WORK", "RecentUnit",\n"Last 3 month unit sales sold", '', rc);\n```	Insert the data into the SAS package. **RecentUnit** is the data table that is forwarded to the packaged results.
```\ncall package_publish(pid, "TO_ARCHIVE", rc,\n"archive_path, archive_name,archive_fullpath"\n,"&temploc", "RecentUnitSales", path);\n```	Publish the package to the temporary physical path indicated by the &TempLoc variable.
```\ncall symput('_ARCHIVE_FULLPATH', path);\ncall package_end(pid, rc);\nrun;\n```	Close the package.
~~%stpend;~~	Do not include %STPBEGIN and %STPEND macros.

Registering the Stored Process

Follow these steps to register the stored process with the SAS Metadata Server.

1. For Server Type, select **Default Server** or **Stored Process Server Only**. The SAS Workspace Server will not work in this example.

2. Select the **Package** result capability.

3. Define a Region prompt with a static selection list and select a default region. In the following window, the East region is the default value for the static list.

#35 You must select a default value for required prompts in order to create the Indicator Data in SAS BI Dashboard successfully.

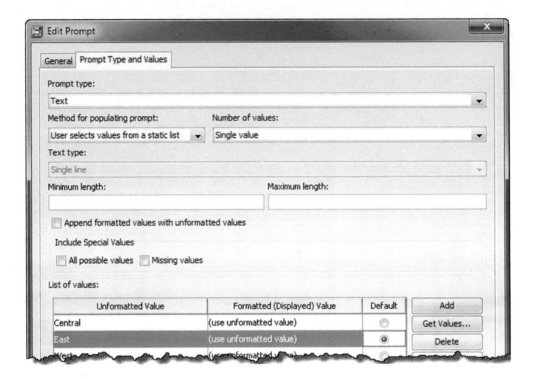

Creating the Dashboard

When adding the data to the SAS BI dashboard, you must set up an indicator that contains the stored process and makes it available as data for the other indicators. This example shows you how to add the stored process and add it to the dashboard.

1. From the SAS BI Dashboard, create an indicator for the stored process.

   a. Select the **New Indicator Data** wizard. When prompted, type the indicator data name, such as DATA_3MonthUnitSalesTotal.

   b. From the Data source drop-down, select **Stored processes**.

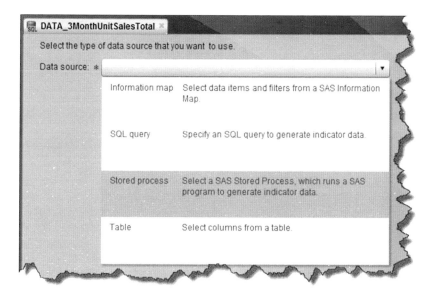

c. Click **Browse** to navigate to the stored process location.

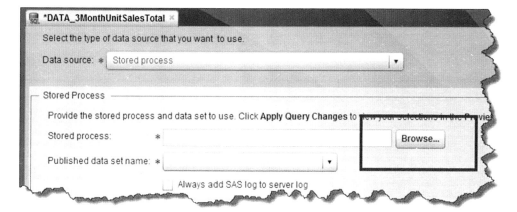

The stored process executes immediately. Review the result by clicking the **Query Results** tab. Because it is the prompt's default selection, the stored process returned 20 rows from the East region. You can view data from each division.

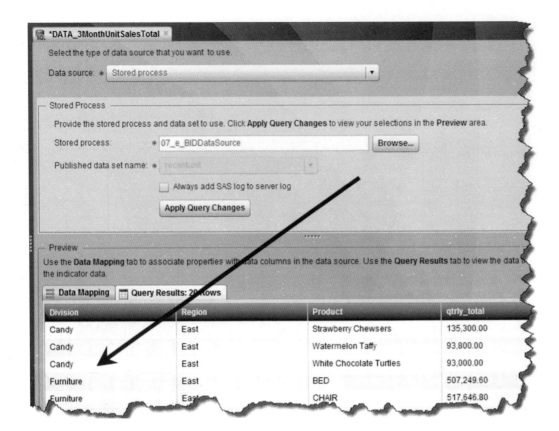

d. Save the indicator data using the **Save** icon.

2. Create a Spark table indicator called IND_3MonthSalesTotals. Use the DATA_3MonthUnitSalesTotal as the Indicator data source.

3. Create a dynamic prompt indicator called IND_RegionPrompt that contains the three regions.

For DATA_Regions Indicator Data, use the SQL query as the Data source and use a query such as: select distinct region from BOOKSAMP.SALESDETAIL2011.

4. Add a Dashboard called Average Quarterly Sales Report. Place the IND_RegionPrompt and the IND_3MonthSalesTotals on the dashboard. The result should be similar to the following figure.

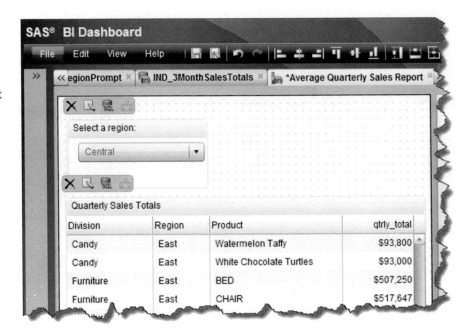

5. Define an interaction between these two indicators so that when a user selects a region, the spark table displays the correct data.

   a. Select **IND_RegionPrompt** and click the **Interactions** icon.

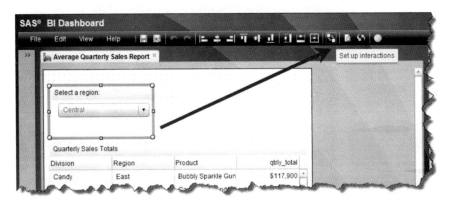

   b. In the Set Up Indicator Interactions window, use the Region prompt as the source indicator. Note that **Source Indicator** drop-down shows the prompt display text instead of indicator name.

   c. In the Available Target Indicators area, choose the **Filter data on remote server** as Interaction Type. Then, select **Region** as the value for Source Data and Target Data.

6. Save the dashboard. When you view the dashboard, it should appear similar to Figure 8-1.

8.1.2 Creating Custom Dashboard Indicators

The SAS BI Dashboard provides a wide range of indicators, and you can increase the list of available graphs by using a stored process. In this scenario, the Candy Company wants to view the current stock price distribution of its company compared to two competitors.

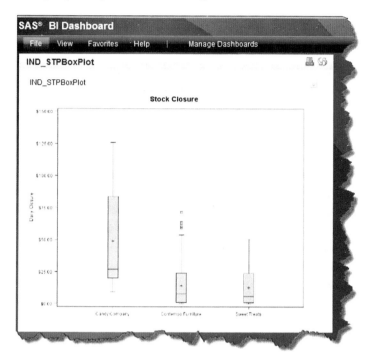

Figure 8-2 Box plot for stock charts

Create a New Stored Process

The BI Dashboard does not have a box plot indicator so a stored process is required to accomplish the executives' requirements.

Example 8-B BID Data Indicator	Notes
`goptions gsfname=_webout` `        gsfmode=replace device=png;`	Do NOT include the %STPBEGIN and %STPEND macros. Set the graphic options.

`libname booksamp meta`
`   library="STP Book Sample Data";`
`title1 'Stock Closure';`
`proc boxplot data=booksamp.stocks;`
`   plot AdjClose*Stock/`
`      boxstyle = schematic`
`      nohlabel;`
`  label AdjClose = 'Daily Closure';`
`  format stock $company.;`
`run;`
	Use the BOXPLOT procedure to create the graph.
	
	Note: Use the BOOKSAMP.STOCKS dataset for this sample. In this example, we used a user-defined custom format ($company.) to convert the company names in the sample dataset to potential competitors.

Registering the Stored Process

When you register the stored process, use the settings in the following steps.

1. From the SAS Management Console, register the stored process.

2. In Execution tab, make the following selections:

   a. In the Server type area, select **Default Server** or **Stored Process Server Only**. The SAS Workspace Server does not work for this example.

   b. In the Result capabilities area, select the **Stream** checkbox.

Adding the Stored Process to the Dashboard

Follow these steps to add this stored process to the dashboard.

1. Use the _action=tree function (described in Section 5.1.1, "Taking Action on the URL") to generate the URL path for the stored process. Keep this URL path in a temporary location for use in step 2b below.

```
http://MachineName:PortNumber/SASStoredProcess/do?_program=%2FProjects%2FBooks%2FSTP+Book%2F08_b_
BIDIndicator&_action=update%2Cnobanner&_updatekey=21828563
```

2. From SAS BI Dashboard, perform the following steps:

   a. Create a new indicator called IND_STPBoxPlot. Select **Custom graph** as the Display type, and leave the other fields empty.

   b. Paste the stored process URL path from step 1 in the **Image Web address** field.

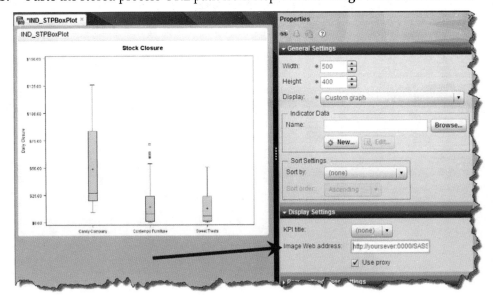

8.2 SAS Information Delivery Portal

The SAS Information Delivery Portal acts as a central interface for all SAS created reports whether built from SAS Enterprise Guide as deployed packages, SAS Stored Processes, or SAS Web Report Studio reports. There are two ways to include a SAS Stored Process Report directly from a portal page: using a Stored Process portlet or using the stored process URL in a URL Display Portlet.

The Candy Company wants to create an Executive Reporting page that includes content from earlier examples. The executive team can access everything from one location.

8.2.1 Using a Stored Process Portlet

The Candy Company wants to add the stock price comparison box plots (created in Section 8.1.2, "Creating Custom Dashboard Indicators") to the portal as a Stored Process portlet.

1. In the SAS Portal, add a new page called Executive Reporting and add a Stored Process Portlet.

2. In the Stored Process Portlet, click **Edit Content**.

3. Make the following changes to the portlet:

    a. In the **Portlet title** field, type **Stock Price Comparison**.

    b. In the **Selected stored process** field, navigate to the Box Plot stored process created in Section 8.1.2, "Creating Custom Dashboard Indicators".

4. Click **OK** to view the box plot in the Executive Report page.

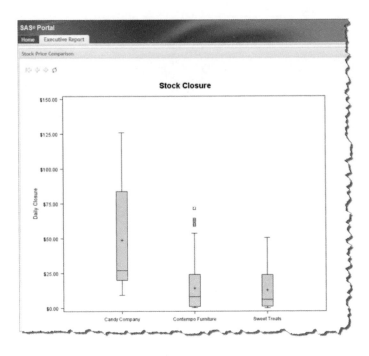

8.2.2 Using a URL Display Portlet

The Candy Company has now asked that the stored process (created in Section 11.1.1, "Adding JavaScript to a Stored Process") with the prompt to the left of the BarLine chart be included in a Sales Report page. You can use a URL Display portlet to display the stored process.

1. Use the _action=tree function to generate the URL path for the stored process. Keep this URL path in a temporary location for use in step 4.

2. Create a Sales Report portal page.

3. Add a URL Display portlet named Predicted and Actual Comparison Report. Return to the SAS Information Delivery Portal home page.

4. Edit the Predicted and Actual Comparison Report portlet by selecting **Edit Content**.

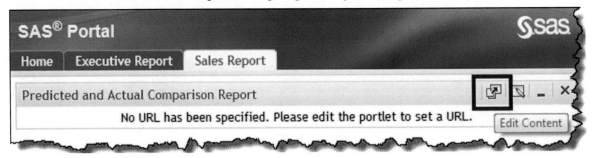

Follow these steps to set the URL path:

a. Paste the URL path from step 1 into the URL field. Remove the &_action and &_updatekey elements.

```
http://MachineName:PortNumber/SASStoredProcess/do?_program=/Projects/11_a_SinglePagePromptsGr
aphs&_action=update%2Cnobanner&_updatekey=1275542093
```

b. Modify the URL so that it uses the SAS Portal web application instead of the SAS Stored Process web application.

`http://`*`MachineName:PortNumber`*`/SASPortal/`~~`SASStoredProcess/do?`~~`_program=/Projects/11_a_SinglePagePromptsGraphs`

c. Add the STPRun directive to the beginning of the URL so that users are not asked to log in again. Your final URL path should resemble the following path:

`http://`*`MachineName:PortNumber`*`/SASPortal/`**`Director?_directive=STPRun&`**
`_program=/Projects/11_a_SinglePagePromptsGraphs`

#36   If parameters are included in the URL, use _directive=STPRunParameters instead of _directive=STPRun.

d. Change the Content Height from 350 to 700 to remove the automatic scroll bar in the view.

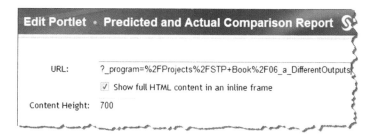

5. Click **Save** and review the resulting stored process in the portlet.

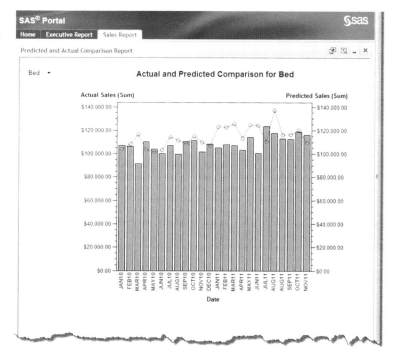

Improving Stored Process Performance

After you have developed multiple stored processes for your users, their next request is often how they can achieve these results faster. Taking time to make prompt selections is one thing, but they want the computer to return immediate results. To accomplish this, SAS offers various functions to improve use and system interaction times.

In this chapter, you will learn how to work with the SAS Stored Process Reports, use background processing, prevent errors before they occur, and use sessions to store data.

9.1 Using Background Processing

One way to manage stored processes that take a long time to complete is to allow the process to run in the background. Running stored processes in the background improves the user's experience, because they no longer receive Web-server timeout error messages, but instead see a background process completed alert in the SAS Information Delivery Portal.

In Section 5.1.1, "Taking Action on the URL" you learned how to use the _action parameter to control how the stored process executed. Another _action option is BACKGROUND.

You can add the _action=BACKGROUND parameter to the stored process as a hidden prompt; however, because it is hidden, you must have a least one other visible prompt or the stored process server will not process it.

 #37 **When using hidden prompts in your stored process, ensure that there is at least one visible prompt so that SAS includes all prompts when the stored process runs.**

For this example, a stored process is needed once a week after some other event, such as the analyst completing a data validation. This unpredictable need makes the stored process difficult to schedule. As an alternative, have the user start the stored process manually after the completing the data validation. However, because the stored process takes a long time to complete and no one needs the results immediately, you decide to run the stored process in the background.

Following these steps to cause the stored process to run in the background:

1. Open the stored process that you want to update.

2. Verify that the stored process generates permanent results. Stored processes which generate a package containing data would be a good candidate, while a stored process with streaming output to a Webpage does not as there is no mechanism to locate the results upon completion.

3. Ensure that the stored process has at least one other visible prompt.

4. Add the _action prompt from the Parameters window. In the New Prompt window, do the following:

    a. In the General tab, type _action in the Name and Displayed text fields.

    b. Select the Hide at run time checkbox.

    c. In the Prompt Type and Values tab, type BACKGROUND in the Default value field.

    d. Click OK to continue.

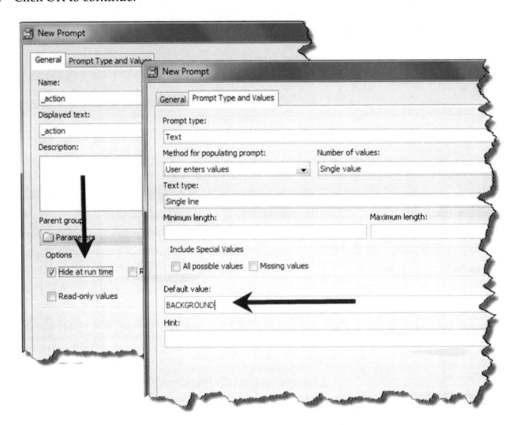

5. Test the stored process to ensure that it run in the background as expected. If working properly, the stored process generates a message similar to the following:

#38 When setting up a stored process to run in the background, ensure that the process outputs to a package or produces a permanent file or data table.

Use the SAS Information Delivery Portal to check the stored process status through an Alert portlet. You can also access the stored process package results from the Alert portlet as well. The Stored Process Alerts Portlet displays all of the completed stored processes that ran in the background and that created package results. If you click on the stored process name, you can see the result. Other actions are available, such as adding a bookmark and publishing or emailing the result. Alerts appear when the stored process has finished executing and generated a transient or permanent package.

 #39 Use the Stored Process Alert Portlet in SAS Information Delivery Portal to receive information on stored processes execution completion.

9.2 Creating Stored Process Reports

Starting in SAS 9.3, developers can create stored process reports, which are essentially cached report results that require no server processing. This function is particularly useful when users request complex reports that require more processing time. In the first release of SAS 9.3, Stored Process Reports are only accessible from the SAS Stored Process Web Application.

In this example, you will create a stored process report for the Actual and Predicted Comparison Chart for a specific product (seen in Example 11-C Output Destination Report).

1. From the SAS Management Console, navigate to the folder where you want to store the report. Right-click the folder name and select **New > Stored Process Report**.

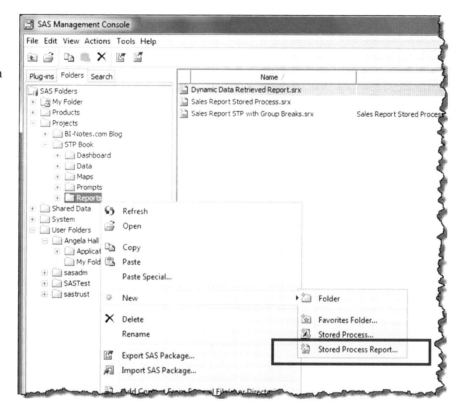

2. Complete the New Stored Process Report window with as much detail as you want. Click **Next** to continue.

3. Follow these steps to add the stored process.

   a. From the Stored Process field, click **Select** to navigate to the stored process that you want to use. You can use stored processes that create packaged results only.

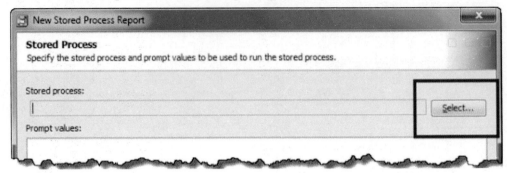

   b. After the stored process loads, you are allowed to add default values for the prompts.

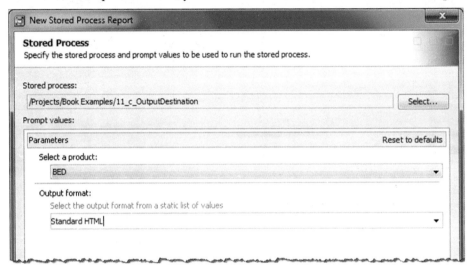

4. In the Output window, modify the maximum number of retained reports and set an expiration policy. In this example, we are storing the last four reports that were created, and each new report is generated on Saturday mornings at 3 AM Eastern time.

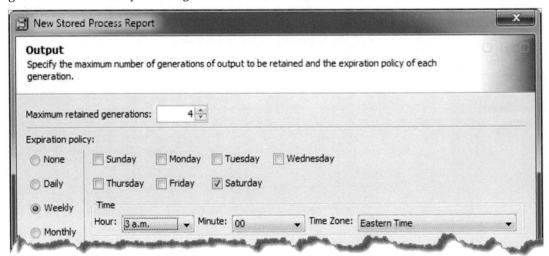

 **#40** **Set expiration dates to remove old Stored Process Reports automatically, reducing overall space requirements.**

After selecting **Finish** on the Output window, the first report is generated when the user selects the report from the Web. To manage the stored process report, right click on the report name in SAS Management Console and choose **Properties**. On the **Output** tab, you can view who created the last report, as well as delete prior caches.

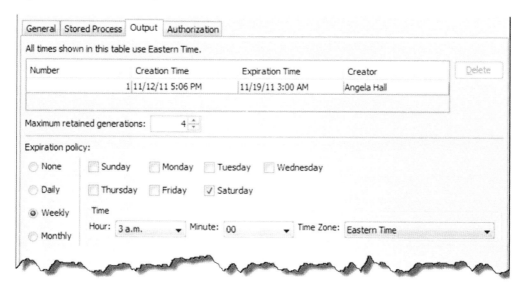

Figure 9-1 Updating Stored Process report schedules

9.3 Using Sessions

When users drill from one report to the next using the same data query, it makes sense to use a session rather than query the same data table again. A session maintains the data libraries (including WORK) and all macro variables between each stored process request. The session can be referenced by a session id value and it expires after a defined timeframe rather than immediately shutting down when the query completes and returns results.

Recall that in Section 1.2.3, "Understanding Server Types" this functionality is only available from the SAS Stored Process Server.

 #41 **Use a session to hold temporary datasets that can be accessed multiple times. This ensures the user has the fastest processing speed.**

For example, a source table is filtered with the first stored process and each additional stored process request (by default) kicks off a new user session rerunning the same filter process. When stored processes build upon each other further refining the data table results or reusing the previous content, it makes sense to use sessions.

Enabling sessions allows you to reuse the first data query in subsequent stored process requests because you are turning off the new user session for a particular user. This can significantly improve processing speed when reusing the same data table in multiple requests.

In Section 3.3, "Chaining Reports" we created two reports to generate a summary and a detail data table. To improve the performance of this report, we could create a user session where the data is filtered by common variables first (in this case, date range) and the filtered table is available for use by subsequent reports.

9.3.1 Update the Summary Report

Begin with the Example 3-D Linked Reports and make the following changes.

Example 9-A Linked Session	Notes
``data _null_;
if libref('SAVE') ne 0
then rc = stpsrv_session('create');
run;```	If the SAVE library does not exist, create a session that will use the stored process.
``%let save_sale_date_min = &sale_date_min;
%let save_sale_date_max = &sale_date_max;```	Copy the two date macros into the session so we can include them in the linked report title.
``%macro query;
libname booksamp meta library="STP Book Sample Data";
proc sql;
create table save.shrdat as
select distinct
state label="State"```	Note that the data table was modified to save.shrdat. That will automatically save the table shrdat in the WORK session for future use.
``propcase(product) as product label="Product"
,product
,prodtype
,date
,country
,predict
,actual``` | Include the other values in the saved session table for use in the report's statistic summary and in the detail report.

Note that the propcase for product was removed so that future filtering on the table would leverage the same uppercase prompt values as seen previously. |
| ```,sum(predict) as predictsum
 label="Total Predicted" format=dollar12.
,sum(actual) as actualsum
 label="Total Actual" format=dollar12.
,sum(predict)-sum(actual) as diff
 label="Variance" format=negparen10.,
 "<a
href='http://&_srvname:&_srvport/SASStoredProcess/do?_act
ion=EXECUTE%nrstr(&_program)=&_metafolder.Sales+Detail2%n
rstr(&sale_date_min)=&sale_date_min%nrstr(&sale_date_max)
=&sale_date_max"
||%nrstr(&prodprompt)="||strip(product)||"%nrstr(&state)=
"||strip(state)||"'>Detailed Report</a>"
as URLLink label="Link"``` | Move the calculations into the summary data generated specifically for this report. |
| ```from booksamp.prdsal2011``` | |

Example 9-A Linked Session	Notes
`where "&date_range_min"d <= date <= "&date_range_max"d`	
~~and upcase(product) in~~ ~~(%if &prodprompt_count = 1~~ ~~%then %do;~~ ~~"&prodprompt"~~ ~~%end;~~ ~~%else %do i = 1 %to~~ ~~&prodprompt_count;~~ ~~"&&prodprompt&i."~~ ~~%end;)~~ ~~%if %length(&state) > 0 %then %do;~~ ~~and state = "&state"~~ ~~%end;~~ ~~group by state, product~~ ~~order by state~~ ~~;~~	Move the additional filtering into the summary data generated specifically for this report.

`create table work.qresult as`
`select distinct`
`  state`
` ,product`
` ,sum(predict) as predictsum`
`    label="Total Predicted" format=dollar12.`
` ,sum(actual) as actualsum`
`    label="Total Actual" format=dollar12.`
` ,sum(predict)-sum(actual) as diff`
`    label="Variance" format=negparen10.`
` ,"<a`
`href='http://&_srvname:&_srvport/SASStoredPro`
`cess/do?_action=EXECUTE%nrstr(&_program)=&_me`
`tafolder.Sales+Detail2"`
`||"%nrstr(&_sessionid)=&_sessionid.%nrstr(&pr`
`odprompt)="||strip(product)||"%nrstr(&state)=`
`"||strip(state)`
	The next step creates a subset of information based on the other prompt selections and includes specific measures for the report.

~~%nrstr(&sale_date_min)=&date_range_min%nrstr(&sale_date~~ ~~_max)=&sale_date_max"~~	When the date range macros are stored as saved macros, the values are included with the session, and they are not required in the URL.
`%nrstr(&_sessionid)=&_sessionid."`	Add &_SESSIONID to the URL. This code passes the created session information to the next stored process when a link is selected off the report. This ensures that the session is reused and that all data and macro variables are included.
`||"'>Detailed Report</a>"`	

Example 9-A Linked Session	Notes

```
as URLLink label="Link"
```

```from save.shrdat``` ```where```	Select from the data saved in the user's session.

```
  product in
(%if &prodprompt_count = 1
 %then %do;
            "&prodprompt"
 %end;
 %else %do i = 1 %to
 &prodprompt_count;
        "&&prodprompt&i."
 %end;
)
  %if %length(&state) > 0 %then %do;
  and state = "&state"
  %end;
  group by state, product
  order by state
;
quit;
title1 'Predicted vs Actual Report';
%if %length(&state) = 0 %then %do;
  title2 height=1 'State, Product';
%end;
%else %do;
  title2 "&state";
  title3 height=1 'Product';
%end;
%if "&graph" = "Yes" %then %do;
  %if "&graphtype" = "PLOT" %then %do;
  proc &graphtype data=work.qresult;
   &graphtype product*&varible;
  run; quit;
  %end;
  %else %do;
  proc gchart data=work.qresult;
   &graphtype &variable;
  run; quit;
  %end;
%end;
proc print data=work.qresult label noobs;
var
  %if %length(&state) = 0 %then %do;
    state
  %end;
    product predictsum actualsum diff urllink;
run;
%mend query;
%STPBEGIN;
options mprint mlogic;
 %query;
%STPEND;
```

9.3.2 Updating the Linked Report

The linked report requires a few modifications in order to use the information that was saved within the session (specified by the &_sessionid included in the URL link).

Example Sales Detail2	Required Modifications
```%let sale_date_min = &save_sale_date_min;``` ```%let sale_date_max = &save_sale_date_max;```	Retrieve the saved date range macros. Note that this change could have been made only in the title line for this particular report.

```%macro query;```
```libname booksamp meta library="STP Book Sample Data";```
```proc sql;```
```create table qresult as select *```
```from save.shrdat```
~~```booksamp.prdsal2011```~~
	Switch the source table with the new saved session table that includes the data from the date range selected

```where``` ~~```"&date_range_min"d <= date <= "&date_range_max"d```~~ ~~```and```~~	Remove the date range prompt query; it is not required.

```
    product in
    ("&prodprompt")
  %if %length(&state) > 0 %then %do;
    and state = "&state"
    %end;
order by state;
quit;
title1 "Detail Report from &SALE_DATE_MIN to
&SALE_DATE_MAX";
%if %length(&state) = 0 %then %do;
  title2 height=1 'State, Product';
%end;
%else %do;
  title2 "&state";
  title3 height=1 'Product';
%end;
proc print data=work.qresult label noobs;
  var date country state prodtype product actual predict;
run;
%mend query;
%STPBEGIN;
options mprint mlogic;
 %query;
%STPEND;
```

9.4 Smart Messaging

When developing code, programmers can use some tricks to quickly review code and address issues before the end-user encounters a problem. Another good development technique is to anticipate user interactions and code for those events so that users never realize an issue exists.

Although it is not possible to code all prompts to ensure that relevant data exists, you can take actions to help prevent some issues. For example, when a user selects an invalid prompt combination and the chart has no resulting data to work with, the user sees a Stored Process Error. To avoid this outcome, add a validation checkpoint within the stored process and send appropriate messages to the user based on the selection.

 #42 If a query fails the dataset will not exist. Test for both scenarios (no records in an existing dataset and no dataset at all) and generate different messages accordingly.

Within Section 2.3, "Using Date Prompts" we created a stored process that allows users to choose a date range along with a product value. If the user selects a date range that has no values, the window is returned as blank.

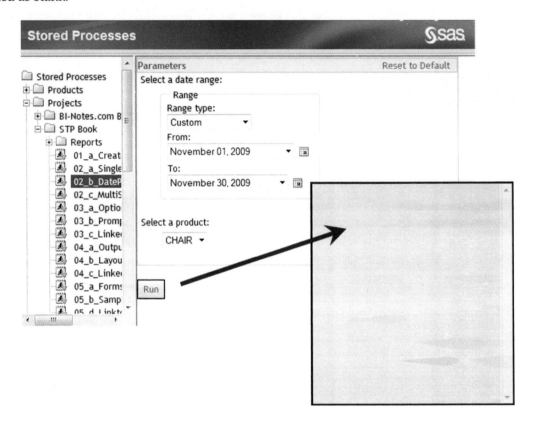

Figure 9-2 Blank result for missing values

Of course, returning a blank window confuses the user. Consider adding a quick check within the code and returning a response that provides more value, so you can avoid user complaints. In the example below, Example 2-B Date Prompts is updated to test for records.

Example 9-C Smart Message	Notes
`%macro query;`	Because we will use conditional logic to determine whether if the data query returns values, the entire step is included within a program macro.

```
libname booksamp meta library="STP Book Sample
Data";
proc sql noprint;
```

Example 9-C Smart Message	Notes
| ```
create table work.qresult as
select distinct state label="State",
propcase(product) as product label="Product",
sum(predict) as predictsum
label="Total Predicted" format=dollar12.,
sum(actual) as actualsum
label="Total Actual"  format=dollar12.
,sum(predict)-sum(actual) as diff
    label="Variance" format=negparen10.
  from booksamp.prdsal2011
    where "&sale_date_min"d <= date <=
"&sale_date_max"d
      and product = "&prodprompt"
group by state, product
order by state;
``` | |
| ```
quit;
%STPBEGIN;
%if &sqlobs > 0 %then %do;
quit;
``` | Test for the number of SQL observations returned from the SQL query by using the automatic macro variable &sqlobs. Note that this macro is accessible only while within the PROC SQL statement. |
| ```
title1 'Predicted vs Actual Report';
title2 height=1 'State, Product';
``` | |
| ```
%end;
%else %do;
select min(date) format=date9.
      ,max(date) format=date9.
into :mindate, :maxdate
from booksamp.prdsal2011; quit;
``` | If no observations are returned (&sqlobs=0), then the actual date minimum and maximum values are retrieved from the data and are included in the message to the user. |
| ```
data qresult;
format Error $45.;
Error='Date Range Selected Returned
0 Values';
    output;
Error="Current Data Between &mindate
and &maxdate";
    output;
run;
%end;
``` | The qresult table includes two messages, one states that 0 records were returned and one includes what date range is available within the data using the minimum and maximum values retrieved above. |
| ```
proc print data=work.qresult label noobs;
run;
``` | Print the qresult table. |
| ```
%mend;
%STPBEGIN;
%query;
``` | Close the program macro, then run the macro within the STPBEGIN and STPEND output macros. |
| ```
%STPEND;
``` | |

In the following figure, you can see the results after the modifications.

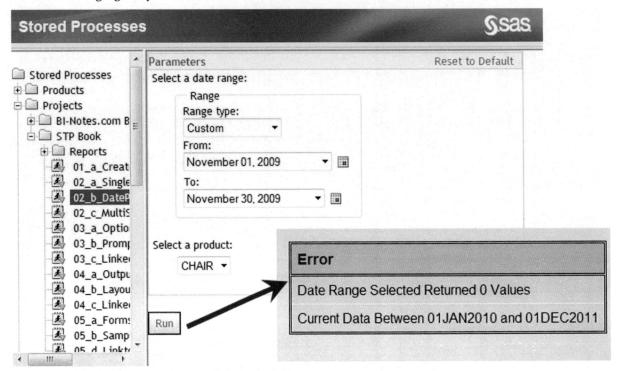

Figure 9-3 Showing the modifications

Creating Custom Interfaces

In prior examples, we relied on the layouts and prompting interfaces available automatically from the SAS system. With any Web browser-friendly code, you can further extend the capabilities of your stored processes. By combining HTML and JavaScript code in a stored process, you can develop your own Web applications.

In this chapter, you will learn different customization techniques, including how to upload files from the user's system, how to leverage the _WEBOUT stream to generate different content types, and how to include JavaScript to collect user input through a customized form. These custom interfaces exponentially increase the capabilities of SAS and stored processes.

10.1 Programming with HTML Code

A common way to collect user input is to solicit information in a Web form. In previous chapters, the prompting framework generated the available forms automatically; however, users frequently request custom forms to meet specific requirements.

In the following simple form, the user types a value and clicks **Submit**. After the user submits the form, the SAS stored process captures the input and takes an action. At first glance, you might think this is another SAS system prompt; however, this example is built from a SAS Stored Process that writes HTML code to build the page. Subsequently the user input is received and processed as a macro variable within the stored process.

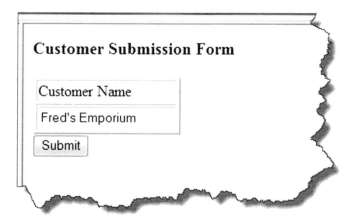

Figure 10-1 Creating the Customer Submission Form

HTML code is the markup language used to create Web pages. Web browsers read the HTML code and display content to the user. In Section 3.3, "Chaining Reports" the sample stored process used hyperlinks in the raw data with HTML code. From a stored process using HTML code, you can create entire Web pages that collect input and display output.

When running a stored process that produces Web output, the HTML code uses the _WEBOUT fileref, which allows the Web browser to display the output. There are several methods within SAS to write HTML code. In this chapter, we discuss the use of PUT statements, as well as CARD (or DATALINES) INPUT statements within data step programming.

When the HTML code is straightforward and the use of ampersands and quotes is limited, the PUT technique is the simplest mechanism to use. Simply put the HTML code inside quotes, which prevents SAS from trying to interpret the line as SAS syntax. When SAS encounters a PUT statement in code, the line is output directly.

As the HTML code becomes longer and more complex, you will find it becomes more difficult or even confusing when you try to ensure that the code has all of the required quotes. In those instances, use the CARD or DATALINES statements to read the HTML code as raw data.

 #43 You can use PUT statements to add HTML code to a stored process. Many programmers find the CARD method provides a more straightforward approach when working with quoting in the HTML code.

The following table shows how the Customer Submission Form (shown above in Figure 10-1) appears when you use each method. The left column shows the PUT statement method, and the right column shows the Input Cards method.

- Both methods require that the HTML code stream the _WEBOUT ❶ location, which creates the HTML file.

- Each PUT statement uses single or double quotes ❷ around an HTML code line.

- The CARDS method treats the HTML code as raw text and does not require quotes ❸ around each line. This allows you to cut and paste an entire HTML file without making any modifications. You can use CARDS or CARDS4. CARDS4 allows you to have semicolons in the input area and requires four semicolons at the end.

Method 1: PUT Statements	Method 2: Cards/Datalines
| ```
data _null_;




❶ file _webout;
``` | ```
data _null_;
  format infile $char256.;
  input;
  infile = resolve(_infile_);
❶ file _webout;
  put infile;
cards;
``` |
| ```
put "<HTML>";
put "<BODY>";
put "<H3>Customer Submission Form</H3>";
❷
put "<FORM ACTION='&_URL'>";
put "<INPUT TYPE='HIDDEN'
    NAME='_program'
    VALUE='&_PROGRAM'>";
``` | ```
<HTML>
<BODY>
<H3>Customer Submission Form</H3>
❸
<FORM ACTION="&_URL">
<INPUT TYPE="HIDDEN"
  NAME="_program"
  VALUE="&_PROGRAM">
``` |

Method 1: PUT Statements	Method 2: Cards/Datalines

```put "<TABLE BORDER=2>";```
```put "<TR><TD>Customer Name</TD></TR>";```
```put "<TD>";```
```put "<INPUT TYPE=TEXT Name='customer'>";```
```put "</TD></TR>";```
```put "</TABLE>";```
```put "<INPUT TYPE='SUBMIT' VALUE='Submit'>";```
```put "</FORM>";```
```put "</BODY>";```
```put "</HTML>";```
	```<TABLE BORDER=2>```
	```<TR><TD>Customer Name</TD></TR>```
	```<TD>```
	```<INPUT TYPE=TEXT Name="customer">```
	```</TD></TR>```
	```</TABLE>```
	```<INPUT TYPE="SUBMIT" VALUE="Submit">```
	```</FORM>```
	```</BODY>```
	```</HTML>```
	```;```

```run;```	```run;```

10.1.1 Using HTML Code with SAS Data Sets

When adding SAS data to the stored process code, you face a new challenge. While PUT statements allow you insert variables within the code, using INPUT CARDS with variables is not that easy. For example, if you want to indicate the customer's current balance and last payment date from the data table, you would use code similar to the following in the output. Using PUT statements and inserting quote marks, you can mix the HTML code and variables (CURRENT_BALANCE_AMT, LAST PAYMENT_DATE). Note the quote marks around the HTML code.

```
put '<p> Customer Balance:' CURRENT_BALANCE_AMT '</p>';
put '<p> Last Payment:' LAST_PAYMENT_DATE '<p>';
```

Because the CARDS method reads the HTML code as raw data, there is no way to insert the variables. To solve this issue, you can use both methods and alternate between the approaches to realize all the benefits from each method.

In this example, you will create a Web form that allows the user to select a company from a list that you generated from a SAS dataset. The result looks similar to the following figure.

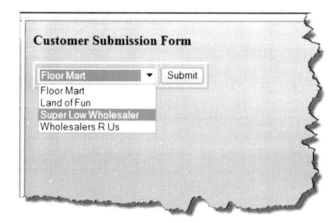

Figure 10-2 Customer Submission Form using both HTML input methods

Using Both HTML Methods

This stored process does use prompts. Notice that the %STPBEGIN/%STPEND macros are not used.

Example 10–A Sample with Both Approaches	Notes
```libname booksamp meta library="STP Book Sample Data";```	Assign the metadata library.
```proc sql; create table CUST_DSN as select distinct name as CUST_NAMES from booksamp.salesdetail2011; quit;```	Use PROC SQL to generate a distinct list of customer names in a column called CUST_NAMES for a work dataset called **CUST_DSN**. This list populates the drop-down form, shown in Figure 10-2.
```data _null_; format infile $char256.; input; infile = resolve(_infile_); file _webout; put infile; cards;```	Use the CARD INPUT method to read in the HTML code. Open the _WEBOUT fileref stream. Throughout this process, we continue writing to this stream.
```<HTML> <BODY BGCOLOR="silver"> <H3>Customer Submission Form</H3> <FORM ACTION="&_URL"> <INPUT TYPE="HIDDEN" NAME="_program" VALUE="&_PROGRAM"> <TABLE BORDER=2> <TR> <TD>```	Use the <HTML> tag to indicate that the HTML file is starting and use the <BODY> tag to place all other HTML code. The &_URL and &_PROGRAM values are assigned at runtime.
```<SELECT Name="CustSelect"> ; run;```	Open a Select list called CustSelect. A Select list allows the data variables to populate in the list. Close the CARDS statement.
```data _null_; set CUST_DSN; file _webout; put ' <OPTION VALUE=" ' cust_value ' "> ' CUST_NAMES ' </OPTION> '; run;```	Start a new data step using the work dataset **CUST_DSN** and continue writing to the _WEBOUT fileref stream. To populate the drop-down list, get the CUST_NAMES variable that you created in the CUST_DSN dataset. The use of quotes is very important here. Each option value must be in quotes, while the dataset variable must be outside of the quotes. When used in the stored process, you can use the CUST_VALUE for processing.
```data _null_; file _webout; put '</SELECT></TD>'; put '<TD>';```	Continue writing to the _WEBOUT fileref stream. Close the Select group.

Example 10–A Sample with Both Approaches	Notes
| ```
put '<INPUT TYPE="SUBMIT"
VALUE="Submit">';
put '</TD>';
put '</FORM>';
put '</BODY>';
put '</HTML>';
run;
``` | Add a Submit button, and then close the FORM and HTML page. |

10.2 Adding Custom Form Options to an Existing Report

Let's return to the customer who requested to link the Predicted vs Actual Report built in Section 3.3, "Chaining Reports". You can improve the report by adding another column so that users can insert comments about the data. The requirement is that the stored process captures the user's name, appends the comment in a permanent dataset, and displays the comment for user review.

Using your new HTML form building skills, you will create a column for the Predicted vs Actual Report. This column allows the user to click an icon in the Add Comments column ❶ that links to a Comment Submission Form. After submitting the comment❷, a confirmation message appears that contains the user's comment.

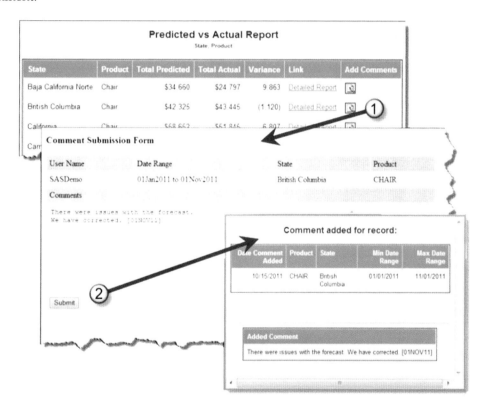

Figure 10-3 Adding a Comment Submission Form with HTML code

Two steps are required to make this stored process work. First, you must create a stored process for the Comment Submission Form. Secondly, you must update the original stored process with the link to the new stored process.
```

10.2.1 Creating the Sales Comment Form Stored Process

The new stored process, Sales Comment Form, uses the following logic:

- When the stored process initially runs, the Comment Submission Form appears, which allows the user to enter comments.

- When the user clicks **Submit**, the stored process determines whether a comment exists. If comment does exist, the process appends the comment to a dataset and displays the Comment Confirmation Notice to the customer. Otherwise, the Comment Submission Form is displayed again.

 #44 When using the _WEBOUT fileref, remove the %STPBEGIN/%STPEND macros and replace them with ODS HTML statements. The ODS HTML statements must include the ODS no_top_matter and no_bottom_matter options.

The following example shows you how to create these two forms and describes the logic that determines which form is displayed. Register this stored process as Sales Comment Form, and place it in the same directory as the Predicted vs. Actual Report stored process.

Example 10-B Sales Comment Form	Notes
`%global submit;`	When the user submits the end form, the &submit macro variable contains a value. We are testing the &submit value to conditionally display the form or the result.

`data html_comment_sub_form;`
`  format infile $char256.;`
`  input;`
`  infile = resolve(_infile_);`
`CARDS;`
 	
`<HTML>`
`<BODY>`
`<H3>Comment Submission Form</H3>`
	Create the Comment Submission Form within the data step using the CARD INPUT method.
	
	Hint: You cannot use CARD statements inside a program macro; you must create the form first.
	
	In the %view macro, this dataset is used.

`<FORM ACTION="&_URL"`
`    method="post"`
`    enctype="multipart/form-data">`
`<INPUT TYPE="HIDDEN"`
`    NAME="_program"  VALUE="&_PROGRAM">`
`<INPUT TYPE="HIDDEN"`
`    NAME="prodprompt" VALUE="&prodprompt">`
`<INPUT TYPE="HIDDEN"`
`    NAME="state" VALUE="&state">`
`<INPUT TYPE="HIDDEN"`
`    NAME="sale_date_min"`
`    VALUE="&sale_date_min">`
`<INPUT TYPE="HIDDEN"`
	The POST method sends the form-data, but it is not shown in the browser's URL. The &_URL and &_PROGRAM values are assigned at runtime. Typically, the URL path must not exceed a certain number of characters, but when using this POST method you are not restricted to a size limit.
	
	The macro variables are called into the INPUT TYPE statements, so that the values can be passed to the stored process when it is submitted.

| Example 10-B Sales Comment Form | Notes |

Code	Notes
| ```
    NAME="sale_date_max"
    VALUE="&sale_date_max">
``` | |
| ```
<table border="0" cellpadding="5">
<tr bgcolor=#D3D3D3>
  <td>User Name</td>
  <td>Date Range</td>
  <td>State</td>
  <td>Product</td>
</tr>
``` | Create an HTML table to hold the form output. |
| ```
<tr bgcolor=#FFFFFF>
  <td>&_username</td>
  <td>&sale_date_min -
&sale_date_max</td>
  <td>&state</td>
  <td>&prodprompt</td>
</tr>
<tr bgcolor=#D3D3D3>
  <td colspan=4>Comments</td>
</tr>
<tr bgcolor=#FFFFFF>
  <td colspan=4>
  <textarea name="comment"
    rows="10" cols="150">
  </textarea>
  </td>
</tr>
``` | The reserved macro variable _username contains the person's name who authenticated with the Web server. |
| ```
<tr><td><input type="submit"
value="Submit"></td></tr>
</table>
</FORM>
</BODY>
</HTML>
;
``` | When the user clicks **Submit**, the reserved macro variable SUBMIT is assigned the value *submit*. |
| ```
run;
``` | |
| ```
%macro view;
``` | Use the %view program macro to analyze the &submit variable to determine which action to take. |
| ```
%if %length(&submit) = 0 %then %do;

  data _null_;
  set html_comment_sub_form;
    file _webout;
``` | If a value is not assigned to the &submit macro variable, the length is null. |
| | The output displays the Comment Submission Form (see Figure 10-3 "Adding a Comment Submission Form |
```

Example 10-B Sales Comment Form	Notes
| ```
    put infile;
  run;

%end;
``` | with HTML code") created in the html_comment_sub_form data step above. |
| ```
%else %do;
%stpbegin;
``` | If the &submit macro does have an assigned value, the stored process uses the %STPBEGIN/ %STPEND macros to display output. |
| ```
libname booksamp meta
library="STP Book Sample Data"
metaout=data;
``` | Assign the library using the META LIBREF type. Use METAOUT=DATA option so that users can write data to the library.<br><br>**Hint:** Metadata must also include authorization for Write/Delete. |
| ```
data newcomment;
attrib
  Comment_Date format=mmddyy10.
    label="Date Comment Added"
  SALE_DATE_MIN format=mmddyy10.
    label="Min Date Range"
  SALE_DATE_MAX format=mmddyy10.
    label="Max Date Range"
  COMMENT
    label="Added Comment"
;
  comment_date=today();
  username="&_username";
  Product="&prodPrompt";
  State="&state";
  sale_date_min="&sale_date_min"d;
  sale_date_max="&sale_date_max"d;
  Comment="&comment";
  run;
``` | Create a new data table called NEWCOMMENT with all the values generated from the form or automatically using the reserved macro variables.<br><br>You can reuse the prompt-value macros from the Predict vs Actual Report. |
| ```
data booksamp.comments;
  set booksamp.comments newcomment;
run;
``` | Update the BOOKSAMP.COMMENTS dataset with the NEWCOMMENT dataset.<br><br>**Note**: Before running this stored process for the first time, create the COMMENTS dataset. We recommend for you to use NEWCOMMENT as the template to initialize BOOKSAMP.COMMENTS. |
| ```
title1 'Comment added for record:';
proc print data=work.newcomment
    label noobs;
  var comment_date product state
``` | Print the NEWCOMMENT dataset to the user as confirmation that the stored process completed successfully. |

Example 10-B Sales Comment Form	Notes
| ```
sale_date_min sale_date_max;
run;

title;
proc print data=work.newcomment label
noobs;
 var comment;
run;
``` | |
| ```
%stpend;
%end;
``` | Close the stored process output and the conditional %IF statement. |
| ```
%mend view;
%view;
``` | Close and run the %View program macro. |

10.2.2 Updating the Linked Report

In Figure 10-1, the Predicted vs Actual Report (created in Section 3.3, "Chaining Reports") has a new column called Add Comments that contains an icon instead of text.

Follow these steps to update the stored process.

1. Upload or locate an image on the Web server.

    In the example, the EditColored.gif image is found in the following folder for jBoss installations:

    <jboss dir>\SASServer1\deploy_sas\sas.storedprocess9.3.ear\sas.storedprocess.war\images

    To link to the image, use the following URL path:

    http://&_srvname:&_srvport/SASStoredProcess/images/EditColored.gif

2. Follow these steps, to update the report to add a new variable that links to the new stored process from the icon.

    a. Copy the URLlink variable and change the name from **URLLink** to **CommentLink.**

    b. Change the stored process from /**Sales+Detail** to /**Sales+Comment+Form**.

    c. Replace the Detailed Report text with the image HTML code, using <img src=> syntax.

        The new variable resembles the following:

        "<a href='http://&_srvname:&_srvport/SASStoredProcess/do?_action=EXECUTE %nrstr(&_program)=/Projects/STP+Book/Books/**Sales+Comment+Form**%nrstr(&sale_date_min)=&sale_date_min%nrstr(&sale_date_max)=&sale_date_max"||"%nrstr(&prodprompt)=" ||strip(product)||"%nrstr(&state)="||strip(state)||"'> **<img src='http://&_srvname:&_srvport/SASStoredProcess/images/EditColored.gif'>**

        </a>" as CommentLink label="Add Comments"

3. Update the PROC PRINT VAR statement to include CommentLink.

The following shows the exact code changes to make.

Example 10-C Summary Report with Comment Link	Notes
| ```
%macro query;
libname booksamp meta library="STP Book Sample Data";
``` | All of the existing SQL query |

Example 10-C Summary Report with Comment Link	Notes
| ```
proc sql;
create table qresult as select distinct
state label="State"
,propcase(product) as product label="Product"
,sum(predict) as predictsum
label="Total Predicted" format=dollar12.
,sum(actual) as actualsum
label="Total Actual" format=dollar12.
,sum(predict)-sum(actual) as diff
label="Variance" format=negparen10.
,"<a
href='http://&_srvname:&_srvport/SASStoredProcess/do?_action=
EXECUTE
%nrstr(&_program)=&_metafolder.Sales+Detail
%nrstr(&sale_date_min)=&sale_date_min
%nrstr(&sale_date_max)=&sale_date_max"
||"%nrstr(&prodprompt)="||strip(product)||"
%nrstr(&state)="||strip(state)||"'>Detailed Report</a>"
as URLLink label="Link"
``` | code remains in place. |

```
,
"<a
href='http://&_srvname:&_srvport/SASStoredProces
s/
do?_action=EXECUTE
%nrstr(&_program)=&_metafolder.
Sales+Comment+Form
%nrstr(&sale_date_min)=&sale_date_min
%nrstr(&sale_date_max)=&sale_date_max"
||"%nrstr(&prodprompt)="||strip(product)
||"%nrstr(&state)="||strip(state)||"'>

<img
src='http://&_srvname:&_srvport/SASStoredProcess
/images/EditColored.gif'>

</a>"

as CommentLink label="Add Comments"
```

Add the CommentLink variable that links to the new stored process and displays the icon.

```
from booksamp.prdsal2011
where "&sale_date_min"d <= date <= "&sale_date_max"d
and    product in
(%if &prodprompt_count = 1
 %then %do;
     "&prodprompt"
 %end;
 %else %do i = 1 %to
 &prodprompt_count;
       "&&prodprompt&i."
 %end;
)
%if %length(&state) > 0 %then %do;
```
```

Example 10-C Summary Report with Comment Link	Notes
| ```
and state = "&state"
  %end;
  group by state, product
  order by state;
quit;
title1 'Predicted vs Actual Report';
%if %length(&state) = 0 %then %do;
  title2 height=1 'State, Product';
%end;
%else %do;
  title2 "&state";
  title3 height=1 'Product';
%end;
%if "&graph" = "Yes" %then %do;
  %if "&graphtype" = "PLOT" %then %do;
  proc &graphtype data=work.qresult;
   &graphtype product*&varible;
  run; quit;
  %end;
  %else %do;
  proc gchart data=work.qresult;
   &graphtype &variable;
  run; quit;
  %end;
%end;
proc print data=work.qresult label noobs;
var
  %if %length(&state) = 0 %then %do;
    state
  %end;
product predictsum actualsum diff urllink
``` | |
| `Commentlink` | Add the new variable. |
| ```
;
run;
%mend query;
%STPBEGIN;
options mprint mlogic;
 %query;
%STPEND;
``` | |

10.3 Uploading Data through a Form

Sometimes you need to collect a file, such as a PDF or comma-separated values (CSV), from the user. Perhaps you are storing the file for later reference or importing the file's contents into a SAS dataset. When using a form to collect the file, the stored process automatically creates a series of _WEBIN reserved macro variables. In this section you will use the stored processes reserved variables to determine whether an attachment was included with the comment and how to store it on the server.

10.3.1 Adding an Attachment

In our sales team example, allowing the team to enter comments has been a big hit at the customer's company. Communication flow between the departments has improved and things are going well. However, the sales team would like to upload attachments for the records. Each salesperson has email messages that are stored as Microsoft Word or PDF documents that contain more information about how they are addressing the variance. Retyping all of this information is inefficient, so the sales staff would like to archive this additional information with the record.

The Comment Submission Form change created in Section 10.2.1, "Creating the Sales Comment Form Stored Process" and seen below, is to add a button that allows the user to upload information to the Comment dataset with the relevant information attached.

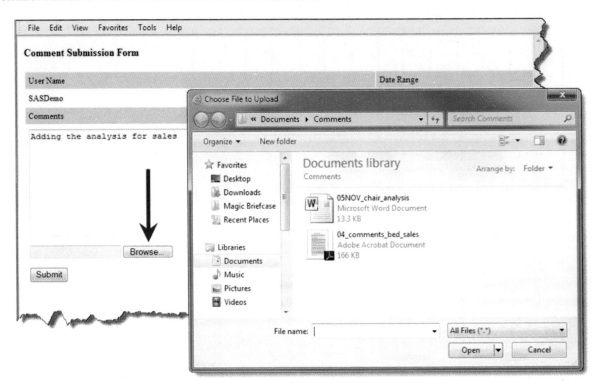

Figure 10-4 Uploading a document to the server

 #45 In HTML forms, use the input type of file (<input name="myfile" type="file" />) to give users a browse button to upload local files into the stored process.

Example 10-D Including Attachments	Notes

<pre>%global submit;
data html_comment_sub_form;
  format infile $char256.;
  input;
  infile = resolve(_infile_);
CARDS;
<HTML>
<BODY>
<H3>Comment Submission Form</H3>
<FORM ACTION="&_URL"
    method="post"</pre>
	No changes are required to this part of the code.

```
    enctype="multipart/form-data">
<INPUT TYPE="HIDDEN"
    NAME="_program"  VALUE="&_PROGRAM">
<INPUT TYPE="HIDDEN"
    NAME="prodprompt" VALUE="&prodprompt">
<INPUT TYPE="HIDDEN"
    NAME="state" VALUE="&state">
<INPUT TYPE="HIDDEN"
    NAME="sale_date_min"
    VALUE="&sale_date_min">
<INPUT TYPE="HIDDEN"
    NAME="sale_date_max"
    VALUE="&sale_date_max">
<INPUT TYPE="HIDDEN"
    NAME="submit"
    VALUE="submitted">
<table border="0" cellpadding="5">
<tr bgcolor=#D3D3D3>
  <td>User Name</td>
  <td>Date Range</td>
  <td>State</td>
 <td>Product</td>
</tr>
<tr bgcolor=#FFFFFF>
  <td>&_username</td>
  <td>&sale_date_min - &sale_date_max</td>
  <td>&state</td>
  <td>&prodprompt</td>
</tr>
<tr bgcolor=#D3D3D3>
  <td colspan=4>Comments</td>
</tr>
<tr bgcolor=#FFFFFF>
  <td colspan=4>
  <textarea name="comment"
     rows="10" cols="150">
     </textarea>
   </td>
</tr>
```

`<tr><td>`
`<input name="attach1" type="file" />`
`</td></tr>`
	Add a field that allows the user to browse their computer for a file.

```
<tr><td><input type="submit" value="Submit"></td></tr>
</table>
</FORM>
</BODY>
</HTML>
;
run;
%macro view;
%if %length(&submit) = 0 %then %do;
  data _null_;
  set html_comment_sub_form;
    file _webout;
    put infile;
```

Example 10-D Including Attachments	Notes
| ```
  run;
%end;
%else %do;
%stpbegin;
``` | |
| ```
%if &_WEBIN_FILE_COUNT > 0 %then %do;
``` | Test for an attachment using the _WEBIN_FILE_COUNT reserved macro variable; if the file exists, then run the steps to store the attachment on the server. |
| ```
%let
UPLOADED=%sysfunc(pathname(&&_WEBIN_FILEREF))
;
data _null_;

PERMLOC="c:\sas\attachments\"
  ||tranwrd(strip(
    scan("&&_WEBIN_FILENAME",
      count("&&_WEBIN_FILENAME"
      , '\')+1
    , '\'))
    , ' ', '_');
rc=rename("&UPLOADED", PERMLOC, 'file');
call symput("attachloc", PERMLOC);
run;
``` | Store the attachment on the server using the _WEBIN_FILEREF reserved macro variable.

There are several methods available through SAS, including PIPE commands.

In this example, the RENAME function copies the file from the work directory into the permanent c:\sas\attachments folder location. |
| ```
%end;
``` | Close the attachment test loop. |

```
libname booksamp meta library="STP Book Sample Data"
metaout=data;
data newcomment;
attrib
  Comment_Date format=mmddyy10.
    label="Date Comment Added"
  SALE_DATE_MIN format=mmddyy10.
    label="Min Date Range"
  SALE_DATE_MAX format=mmddyy10.
    label="Max Date Range"
  COMMENT
    label="Added Comment"
;
  comment_date=today();
  username="&_username";
  Product="&prodPrompt";
  State="&state";
  sale_date_min="&sale_date_min"d;
  sale_date_max="&sale_date_max"d;
  Comment="&comment";
```

| ```
  attachment="&attachloc";
``` | Include the permanent attachment location for user reference. |
```

Example 10-D Including Attachments	Notes
| ```
run;
data booksamp.comments;
 set booksamp.comments newcomment;
run;
title1 'Comment added for record:';
proc print data=work.newcomment label noobs;
 var comment_date product state sale_date_min
sale_date_max;
run;
title;
proc print data=work.newcomment label noobs;
 var comment;
run;
%stpend;
%end;
%mend view;
%view;
``` | |

Other _WEBIN reserved macro variables are available for use. The following example shows what the variables could contain which can help you understand how you could use it in your stored process.

Variable	Definition	Example
_WEBIN_CONTENT_LENGTH	Contains the attached file length in bytes. The Web browser generates this value.	622392
_WEBIN_CONTENT_TYPE	Provides the attach file type (such as pdf or csv). The Web browser generates this value.	application/pdf
_WEBIN_FILEEXT	The file extension. Use this value to validate the file type entering the SAS program.	PDF
_WEBIN_FILENAME	Contains the original file location on the user's machine. Use this value to save the file with the same filename on the server side.	C:\Users\anhall\Desktop\attachmentupload.pdf
_WEBIN_FILEREF	SAS automatically creates a FILEREF for the uploaded file. Use this value with the PATHNAME function to retrieve the temporary file location on the server.	#LN00008
_WEBIN_FILE_COUNT	Counts the number of files uploaded into the program, typically this is used to loop through the reading or copying steps or to determine if a file is uploaded at all.	1
_WEBIN_NAME	Contains the HTML input statement name.	attach1
```

10.4 Adding New Data from Uploaded File

One of our sample sales teams uses a CSV file to store comments. They prefer to upload the CSV file directly into the Comments dataset, rather than copy comments manually for each state and product combination. Automating this process with a stored process would allow users to locate the CSV file❶ on their system, import the file, and append to the dataset❷.

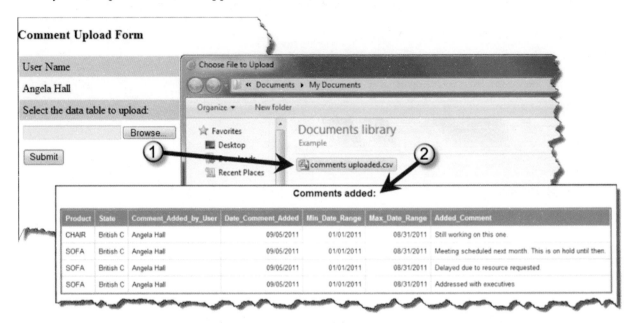

Figure 10-5 Uploading a document to append to a dataset

This particular stored process includes additional logic. For example, if the user tries to upload a non-CSV file, such as a Microsoft Word document (.doc), the stored process prevents this action and alerts the user with this message:

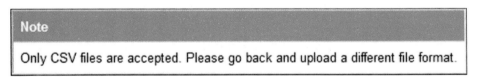

Figure 10-6 CSV procedure error message

10.4.1 Updating the Stored Process Code

Update the Sales Comment Form stored process code from Section 10.2.1, "Creating the Sales Comment Form Stored Process" to display the Browse button only.

Example 10-E Comment Upload Form	Notes

```%global submit;```
 ```data html_comment_sub_form;```
 ``` format infile $char256.;```
 ``` input;```
 ``` infile = resolve(_infile_);```
 ```cards;```
 ```<HTML>```
 ```<BODY>```
	No changes required.

```<H3>Comment Upload Form</H3>```	Rename the title of the form.

```<FORM ACTION="&_URL"```
 ```method="post" enctype="multipart/form-data">```
 ```<INPUT TYPE="HIDDEN" NAME="_program"```
 ```VALUE="&_PROGRAM">```	

```<INPUT TYPE="HIDDEN"```
 ```   NAME="prodprompt" VALUE="&prodprompt">```
 ```<INPUT TYPE="HIDDEN"```
 ```   NAME="state" VALUE="&state">```
 ```<INPUT TYPE="HIDDEN"```
 ```   NAME="sale_date_min"```
 ```   VALUE="&sale_date_min">```
 ```<INPUT TYPE="HIDDEN"```
 ```   NAME="sale_date_max"```
 ```   VALUE="&sale_date_max">```
	Remove the hidden inputs for the sale_date, prodprompt, and state variables. The CSV file contains these variables.

```<INPUT TYPE="HIDDEN" NAME="submit" VALUE="submitted">```
 ```<table border="0" cellpadding="5">```
 ```<tr bgcolor=#D3D3D3>```
 ```<td>User Name</td></tr>```
 ```<tr bgcolor=#FFFFFF> <td>&_username</td></tr>```	

```<tr bgcolor=#D3D3D3>``` ```<td>Select the data table to upload:</td></tr>```	Add text that explains what you want the user to do.

```<tr> <td>```
 ``` <input name="attach1" type="file"/>```
 ```</td></tr>```
 ```<tr> <td>```
 ``` <input type="submit" value="Submit">```
 ```</td></tr>```
 ```</table>```
 ```</FORM>```
 ```</BODY>```
 ```</HTML>```
 ```;```
 ```run;```
 ```%macro view;```
 ```%if %length(&submit) = 0 %then %do;```
 ``` data _null_;```
 ``` set html_comment_sub_form;```
 ``` file _webout;```	

Example 10-E Comment Upload Form	Notes
| ```
   put infile;
  run;
%end;
%else %do;
%stpbegin;
``` | |
| ```
%if "&_WEBIN_FILEEXT" = "csv"
  %then %do;
``` | Test the uploaded file extension to ensure it is a CSV file.<br><br>The reserved macro _WEBIN_FILEEXT shows the file extension. If it is equal to CSV, then the data import step begins. |
| ```
%let UPLOADED=
    %sysfunc(pathname(&&_WEBIN_FILEREF));
proc import datafile="&UPLOADED"
 out=work.newcomment
 dbms=csv
 replace;
 getnames=yes;
run;
``` | We removed the entire data step to create NEWCOMMENT, and we replaced it with the IMPORT procedure. |
| ```
libname booksamp meta library="STP Book Sample Data"
metaout=data;
data booksamp.comments;
 set booksamp.comments newcomment;
run;
title1 'Comments added:';
proc print data=newcomment label noobs; run;
``` | ```
The NEWCOMMENT dataset is then
appended to the BOOKSAMP.COMMENTS
dataset.
Note: More validation statements
could further improve this code. For
example, consider adding code that
ensures the import file contains
valid variables names and lengths.
``` |
| ```
%end;
%else %do;
data notvalid;
Note="Only CSV files are accepted. Please
go back and upload a different file
format.";
run;
proc print noobs; run;
%end;
``` | If the file type is not CSV, inform the user the file type is invalid. |
| ```
%stpend;
%end;
%mend view;
%view;
``` | |
```

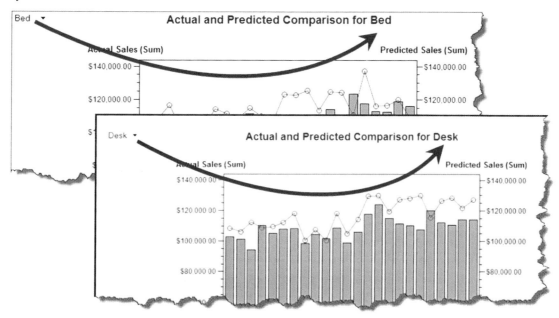

Chapter

11

Generating Custom Output

After grasping the methods to write HTML code directly into the browser, the capabilities of stored processes as Web-based applications become virtually unlimited. In this chapter, you will learn how to add JavaScript to your stored processes, control the output format, and send email messages to mobile devices.

11.1 Combining JavaScript with SAS Procedures

The Furniture Company had a new idea that they want to implement. One of the sales analysts created a chart that the vice president loves. The vice president is not particularly tech-savvy (or patient), so the sales analysts want a page that shows the chart but also allows the user to select a product from a drop-down box, which immediately updates the chart. Using JavaScript, you can implement this type code quickly.

Figure 11-1 Using a drop-down box with a SAS graph

SAS programs use procedures, such as PROC GCHART or PROC REPORT, to generate output. When a SAS procedure is in a stored process, the %STPBEGIN/%STPEND macros ensure that the output displays properly. Using HTML code in a stored process ensures that the output goes to the _WEBOUT file location. The %STPBEGIN macro locks the _WEBOUT location and does not allow other steps within the code from writing to that location. However, there is a way to combine both approaches in a single SAS program - use ODS HTML statements.

You can use ODS HTML code to write to the _WEBOUT fileref location. When you add the no_top_matter or the no_bottom_matter options, the top or bottom tags are suspended. The ODS no_bottom_matter option opens the _WEBOUT location, but it does not write the HTML closing tags automatically. Similarly, the ODS no_top_matter option suppresses the starting tags. Using either or both options allows you to insert custom code, such as JavaScript, to the output stream.

Chapter 10, "Creating Custom Interfaces" contained several examples of using HTML code to generate output. HTML code requires a set of tags to start a Web page (<HTML>, <BODY>) and another set of tags to end the page (</BODY>, </HTML>). Both %STPBEGIN/%STPEND macros and ODS HTML statements write this HTML code for you when creating output. To create the example in Figure 11-1, you must control the creation of the HTML starting and ending tags so that you can use the JavaScript and SAS Procedure together.

#46   To add custom JavaScript code, use the ODS HTML statements with the no_bottom_matter and no_top_matter options to control the _WEBOUT stream.

11.1.1 Adding JavaScript to a Stored Process

The following code creates the stored process shown in Figure 11-1. The first time the stored process runs, it uses a product default value to display the chart. In subsequent applications, the user can select a value from the drop-down menu and the stored process is updated immediately.

Example 11-A Single Page Prompts and Graphs	Notes
`%global prodprompt;`	Create a global macro variable for the default value and user selection.
	The drop-down menu on the top left of the page uses the prodprompt macro variable.
`goptions device=actximg;`	Define the graphics device for PROC GBARLINE. See Section 4.1, "Changing Your Output Appearance" for more information.

`ods html`
`  body=_webout(no_bottom_matter)`
`  style=sasweb`
`  path=&_tmpcat (url=&_replay);`
	Open the _WEBOUT location using an ODS HTML statement. Use the no_bottom_matter option to write the SASWeb style sheet to the stream without writing the closing HTML tags.

`ods html close;`	Close this HTML statement. Because you indicated the no_bottom_matter option, the _WEBOUT stream remains open.
`%macro view;` `data _null_;`	Create the VIEW macro to control what displays on the page.
`file _webout;`	Open the _webout location.

Example 11-A Single Page Prompts and Graphs	Notes
```put '<script type="text/javascript" language="JavaScript">'; put 'function UpdateChart() {'; put 'document.DoubleOut.submit();'; put ' }'; put ' </script>';```	Add the JavaScript code to submit the stored process when the user makes a selection from the drop-down menu. The JavaScript UpdateChart() function automatically submits the DoubleOut form therefore no Run or Submit button is needed.
```put " <FORM NAME='DoubleOut' ACTION='&_URL' method='post' enctype='multipart/form-data'>";```	Add the code to create the drop-down menu. Use the same name (DoubleOut) as specified in the JavaScript document tag above.
```put "<INPUT TYPE='HIDDEN' NAME='_program' VALUE='&_PROGRAM'>"; put '<table border="0" cellpadding="5">';```	
```put '<TR> <TD valign=TOP> <SELECT Name="prodprompt" onChange="UpdateChart();">';```	Create the prodprompt drop-down menu and call the UpdateChart() JavaScript function when the user makes a different selection.
```put '<OPTION VALUE="Bed"'; %if "&prodprompt"="Bed" %then put ' SELECTED '; put '>Bed</OPTION>'; put '<OPTION VALUE="Chair"'; %if "&prodprompt"="Chair" %then put ' SELECTED'; put '>Chair</OPTION>'; put '<OPTION VALUE="Desk"'; %if "&prodprompt"="Desk" %then put ' SELECTED '; put '>Desk</OPTION>'; put '<OPTION VALUE="Sofa"'; %if "&prodprompt"="Sofa" %then put ' SELECTED '; put '>Sofa</OPTION>'; put '</SELECT></TD>';```	Add an option for each product value. This code replaces a prompt. If the &prodprompt macro value was previously selected, the drop-down menu maintains that selection by adding SELECTED to the OPTION tag.
```%if %length(&prodprompt) = 0 %then %do; %let prodprompt=Bed; %end; run;```	If this is the initial run or if &prodprompt is empty, use Bed as the default value.
```ods html```	Use the ODS HTML statement to

Example 11-A Single Page Prompts and Graphs	Notes
| ```
body=_webout(no_top_matter
            no_bottom_matter)
path=&_tmpcat
(url=&_replay);
``` | open the _WEBOUT stream for the PROC statements.<br><br>Use the no_top_matter and no_bottom_matter options to prevent the system from writing HTML starting or ending tags to the_WEBOUT stream.<br><br>**Note**: You specified the style sheet on the first ODS HTML statement. |
| ```
libname booksamp meta library="STP Book
Sample Data";
title1 "Actual and Predicted Comparison
   for &prodprompt";
proc gbarline data=booksamp.prdsal2011;
where
lowcase(product)=lowcase("&prodprompt");
format date monyy5.;
bar date /sumvar=actual;
plot /sumvar=predict;
run;
``` | Add a TITLE statement and use the prodprompt macro variable so that the user knows which product is showing.<br><br>Use a WHERE statement to select the chosen value for the macro variable. |
| ```
ods html close;
``` | Close the ODS output statement. |
| ```
data _null_;
   file _webout;
   put '</TR>';
   put '    </table>';
   put '</FORM>';
   put '</BODY>';
   put '</HTML>';
   run;
%mend view;
%view;
``` | Close the _WEBOUT stream with the HTML closing tags.<br><br><br><br><br><br><br>Run the %view macro. |

11.1.2 Using JavaScript to Manage Other Issues

In Section 10.2, "Adding Custom Form Options to an Existing Report" you created a form to collect comments. This morning, the customer called to let you know that some users were crashing the system when they pasted text into the Comment area. When troubleshooting the issue, you discover that when the user pastes text from sources, such as Microsoft Word, the text might contain special characters, such as line feed or other invisible characters. The SAS Stored Process cannot handle these special characters successfully. When this happens, the system halts all processing.

Attempts to address this issue from within the SAS code fails. When SAS receives the data, it is not readable, so there is no way to clean or change the data using a SAS function. You need a method to clean the pasted text (without the removing characters that you do want) before submitting it into the stored process.

JavaScript can help overcome this issue. When the user submits the text, allow the stored process to send the incoming text through a JavaScript function so that it can convert any special characters into a blank space. Then the text is forwarded into the SAS code for processing. In Figure 11-2, the stored process properly handles the special characters in the output using JavaScript.

Figure 11-2 Working with special characters

This example shows how to update the stored process with JavaScript code.

Example 11—B JavaScript Validation	Notes

```%global submit;```
```data html_comment_sub_form;```
``` format infile $char256.;```
``` input;```
``` infile = resolve(_infile_);```	

~~cards;~~ ```cards4;```	Use the CARDS4 statement when the input code has semicolons, such as JavaScript.

```<HTML>```
```<BODY>```
```<H3>Comment Submission Form</H3>```	

```<script type="text/javascript">```
```function cleartext(form)```
```{test=form.comment.value```
``` test=```
``` test.replace(/[^a-zA-Z 0-9 @.,?!;:()-_]+/g```
```   , " ")```
``` form.comment.value=test```
```}```
```</script>```
	Add a JavaScript code with a CLEARTEXT function. This code takes the COMMENT field value and converts all characters not equal to the values within the brackets (including a-z, A-Z, and 0-9) to a blank space (for example, " ").

Example 11—B JavaScript Validation	Notes

```
<FORM ACTION="&_URL" method="post"
  onsubmit="return cleartext(this)"
enctype="multipart/form-data">
```

Add the FORM tags with the OnSubmit option to run the JavaScript code. OnSubmit calls the ClearText function.

```
<INPUT TYPE="HIDDEN" NAME="_program" VALUE="&_PROGRAM">
<INPUT TYPE="HIDDEN" NAME="prodprompt"       VALUE="&prodprompt">
<INPUT TYPE="HIDDEN" NAME="state"     VALUE="&state">
<INPUT TYPE="HIDDEN" NAME="sale_date_min" VALUE="&sale_date_min">
<INPUT TYPE="HIDDEN" NAME="sale_date_max" VALUE="&sale_date_max">
<INPUT TYPE="HIDDEN" NAME="submit"     VALUE="submitted">
<table border="0" cellpadding="5">
<tr bgcolor=#D3D3D3>
<td>User Name</td>      <td>Date Range</td>
<td>State</td>          <td>Product</td></tr>
<tr bgcolor=#FFFFFF>
<td>&_username</td>     <td>&sale_date_min to &sale_date_max</td>
<td>&state</td>         <td>&prodprompt</td></tr>
<tr bgcolor=#D3D3D3>    <td colspan=4>Comments</td></tr>
<tr bgcolor=#FFFFFF>    <td colspan=4>
<textarea name="comment" rows="10" cols="150">
</textarea></td></tr>
<tr><td><input name="attach1" type="file" /></td></tr>
<tr><td><input type="submit" value="Submit"></td></tr>
</table> </FORM> </BODY> </HTML>
```

```
;
;;;;
```

Add four semicolons to close the CARDS4 statement.

```
run;
%macro view;
%if %length(&submit) = 0 %then %do;
  data _null_;
  set html_comment_sub_form;
    file _webout;
    put infile;
  run;
%end;
%else %do;
%stpbegin;
%if &_WEBIN_FILE_COUNT > 0 %then %do;
  %let UPLOADED=%sysfunc(pathname(&&_WEBIN_FILEREF));
  data _null_;
    PERMLOC="c:\sas\attachments\"||tranwrd(strip(scan("&&_WEBIN_FILENAME",
count("&&_WEBIN_FILENAME", '\')+1, '\')), ' ', '_');
    rc=rename("&UPLOADED", PERMLOC, 'file');
  run;
%end;
libname booksamp meta library="STP Book Sample Data" metaout=data;
  data newcomment;
    format comment_date sale_date_min sale_date_max mmddyy10.;
    comment_date=today();
    username="&_username";     product="&prodprompt"; state="&state";
    sale_date_min="&sale_date_min"d;   sale_date_max="&sale_date_max"d;
    comment="&comment";
    attrib product label="Product";
    attrib state label="State";
```

Example 11—B JavaScript Validation	Notes

```
    attrib comment_date label="Date Comment Added";
    attrib sale_date_min label="Min Date Range";
    attrib sale_date_max label="Max Date Range";
    attrib comment label="Added Comment";
  run;
  data booksamp.comments;
    set booksamp.comments newcomment;
  run;
  title1 'Comment added for record:';
  proc print data=work.newcomment label noobs;
    var comment_date product state sale_date_min sale_date_max;
  run;
  title;
  proc print data=work.newcomment label noobs; var comment; run;
%stpend;
%end;
%mend view;
%view;
```

11.2 Reports in Other Formats

In all of the prior examples, the stored process sent output to a Web browser. However, many users like to share the stored process results in other formats, such as PDF and RTF, or share the output with email clients or mobile devices. Multiple output formats and devices can create new challenges.

11.2.1 Selecting a Destination Output Format

The GBARLINE procedure you created for the vice president in our previous example is gaining popularity in the company. Now the customer wants the user to select from multiple output formats, such as HTML, PDF, and RTF.

In Section 4.1, "Changing Output Appearance" you learned how to use shared prompts with reserved macro variables to control the style and device. There is also a shared prompt for output format, as shown in the following figure. This prompt uses the reserved _ODSDEST to set the output format at run time.

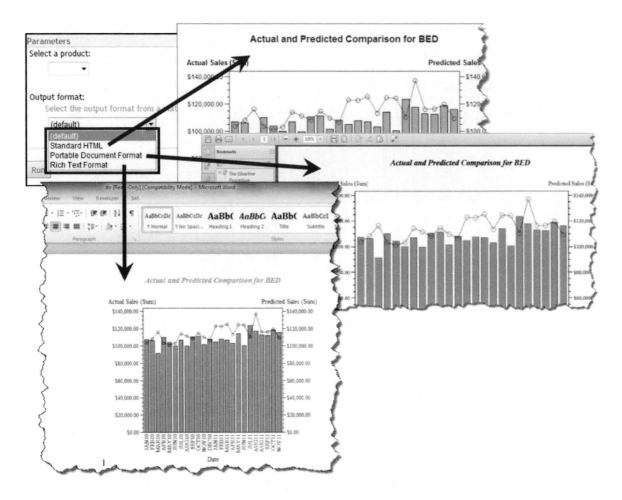

Figure 11-3 Using one prompt to send output to multiple destinations

#47 The stored process reserved macro _ODSDEST and the SAS ODS system option ODSDEST provide two different functions. _ODSDEST affects the current stored process output type while ODSDEST sets the default for all BASE SAS output.

11.2.2 Create the Stored Process Code

Create a new stored process that uses the GBARLINE code from the stored process in Section 11.1.1, "Adding JavaScript to a Stored Process ".

Example 11—C Output Destination	Notes
``%stpbegin;
libname booksamp meta library="STP Book Sample Data";
title1 "Actual and Predicted Comparison for &prodprompt";
proc gbarline data=booksamp.prdsal2011;
where lowcase(product)=lowcase("&prodprompt");
format date monyy5.;
bar date /sumvar=actual;
plot /sumvar=predict;
run;
%stpend;```	Use the %STPBEGIN and %STPEND macro variables to setup the necessary code to automatically produce results in the _ODSDEST selected format.

11.2.3 Register the Stored Process

When you register this stored process, you must create two prompts: one for the product and a second prompt for the _ODSDEST format. See Section 4.1, "Changing Output Appearance" for detailed steps for adding a shared prompt.

Use the following steps to register the stored process:

1. From the SAS Management Console, register the stored process.

2. Select both **Stream** and **Package** Result capabilities on the **Execution** tab.

3. From the Parameters tab, add a text prompt for product called prodprompt.

4. Add a shared prompt for the _ODSDEST variable.

    a. Click **Add Shared**.

    b. Navigate to the Products>SAS Intelligence Platform>Samples folder and select the **ODS Output Format – Static** shared prompt.

    c. When prompted to change the name, select **OK** to keep the current value. The prompt name _ODSDEST corresponds to the reserved macro variable.

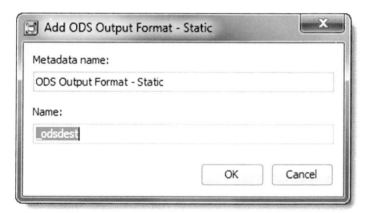

5. Because this is a shared prompt, you cannot make any changes until it is made unshared. Select the prompt, click **Unshare**.

6. When the shared prompt is unshared, the system copies it to the stored process. The system displays a warning message to ensure that this action is what you wanted to do. Select **Yes** to continue.

7. For this prompt, you want to make a distinct list of formats available. Use the following steps to edit the prompt.

    a. From the **Parameters** tab, select the _ODSDEST prompt and click **Edit**. The Edit Prompt window appears.

    b. From the **Prompt Type and Values** tab, select the **chtml** option and click **Delete**. Repeat this step for the **phtml**, **xml,** and **sasreport** options.

    c. Click **OK** to save the changes and exit the window.

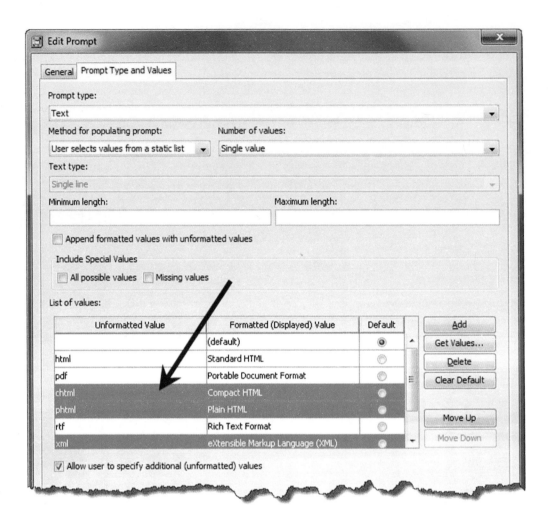

8. Complete the stored process registration and test the results to ensure that it works as expected. Your results should be similar to Figure 11-3.

11.3 Your Report as an Email Message

After observing the users, management realized that the multiple outputs were the first step to emailing the results to the customer. To improve productivity, management quickly made the request to add a prompt in the stored process to insert email addresses and forward the report.

In Figure 11-4, the user selected the product and typed the email address and subject. The stored process sends the chart as a PDF attachment. This stored process uses the FILENAME statement to attach the PDF file and send the email.

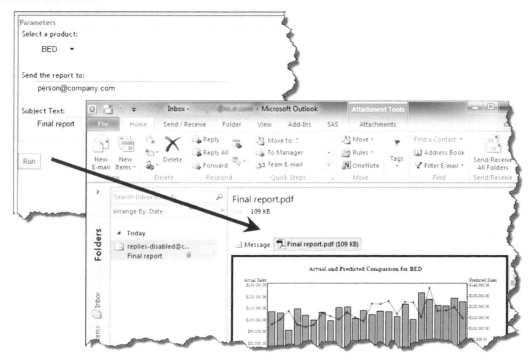

Figure 11-4 Sending email messages from stored processes

11.3.1 Update the Stored Process Code

When you update the stored process, you must remove the _odsdest prompt and create two new text prompts: _EMAIL_ADDRESS and _SUBJECT, as shown in Figure 11-5. These prompts contain the email address and the email subject.

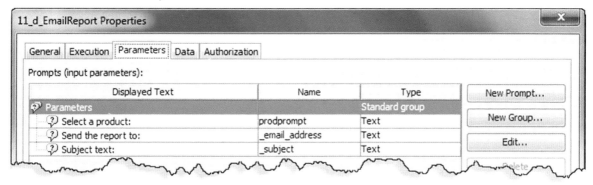

Figure 11-5 Adding prompts for the email macro variables

Update the stored process code to send the email with the PDF attachment.

Example 11—D EmailReport	Notes
| ```
filename pdfout
  EMAIL
  to="&_email_address"
  from="replies-disabled@company.com"
  subject="&_subject"
  content_type='application/pdf';
``` | Define an FILEREF using the prompt macro variables for _SUBJECT and _EMAIL_ADDRESS.<br><br>**Note**: In some organizations, the FROM option might be preset and any value you supply will be ignored. In other cases, the e-mail will not be sent if an invalid from email address is used. |
| ```
%stpbegin;
libname booksamp meta library="STP Book Sample Data";
``` | |
| ```
goptions device=PNG;


ods pdf
  file=pdfout;
``` | Set the device to PNG. Other devices such as JPEG and GIF will also work.<br><br>Wrapped within the %STPBEGIN and %STPEND macros is the ODS PDF statement. This prints the results directly to the PDFOUT FILEREF defined above. |
| ```
title1 "Actual and Predicted Comparison for &prodprompt";
  proc gbarline data=booksamp.prdsal2011;
  where lowcase(product) = lowcase("&prodprompt");
  format date monyy5.;
  bar date /sumvar=actual;
  plot /sumvar=predict;
  run; quit;
``` | |
| ```
ods pdf close;
``` | Close the ODS statement. |
| ```
%stpend;
``` | |

11.3.2 Resizing a Mobile Device Report

Executives at the Furniture Company frequently use their mobile devices to review reports. They have requested that the report fit directly within their mobile device screens rather than as an attached PDF. To accommodate this request, you can control the size of the graphs to create a more readable report.

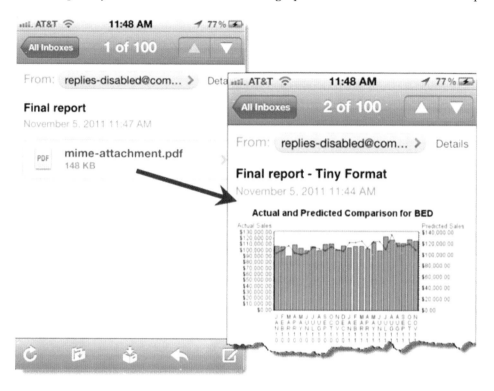

Figure 11-6 Viewing email messages on a mobile device

Note that your email system might handle PDF attachments differently, either as an attachment or as a viewable item via the email application itself.

 #48   You can adjust report margins. The VSIZE and HSIZE values depend on how many graphs you want to print on one page. You might need to try several different settings to achieve the best results.

To update the stored process, you need to change the output format and method. Use the GOPTIONS statement to temporarily set default values for graphic attributes. Refer to SAS Support Site (http://support.sas.com) for more information about the available GOPTIONS options.

Example 11—E TinyEmail	Notes
`ods listing;`	Use the ODS LISTING statement when you want to print graphics to a specific location.
	Note: In SAS 9.3, this option is set to off by default.

Example 11—E TinyEmail	Notes

```
filename gout EMAIL
  to="&_email_address"
  from="replies-disabled@company.com"
  subject="&_subject"
  content_type='application/pdf'
content_type='image/gif';
```

Change the content_type to output to GIF format to control output with the GOPTIONS statements.

```
%stpbegin;
goptions device=PNG;
ods pdf file=pdfout;
goptions reset=all dev=gif
  gsfname=gout gsfmode=replace
  ypixels=300   xpixels=500;
```

Add the GOPTIONS statement and set the device as GIF.

Use the YPIXELS and XPIXELS options to control the height (y-axis) and width (x-axis) of the graphics output.

```
libname booksamp meta library="STP Book Sample Data";
title1 "Actual and Predicted Comparison for &prodprompt";
  proc gbarline data=booksamp.prdsal2011;
  where lowcase(product) = lowcase("&prodprompt");
  format date monyy5.;
  bar date /sumvar=actual;
  plot /sumvar=predict;
  run; quit;
```

```
filename gout clear;
ods listing close;
ods pdf close;
%stpend;
```

Close the graphics and listing output locations.

11.3.3 Ensuring Email Options Setup

During installation and configuration, the SAS administrator defines a connection to a SMTP server. If you are unable to send email messages from the stored process, verify that the configuration is complete by running the following code from BASE SAS or SAS Enterprise Guide:

```
proc options group=email; run;
```

The resulting log should include your SMTP server for EMAILHOST and EMAILPORT options. If these options are not set or you cannot send an email, contact your SAS administrator for assistance.

Chapter

12

Using PROC STP

As seen throughout this book, one of the most significant benefits of using SAS stored processes is it's extendibility. Setting up reports that can run from different client interfaces, enhancing out-of-the-box functionality with custom widgets, and leveraging the various SAS Stored Process Server options makes this component one of the most customizable products from SAS.

In SAS Version 9.3, SAS introduced the STP procedure, which allows you to execute the stored process code from other stored processes or within a SAS session. This adds another mechanism to the extensive list of client interfaces from which stored processes can be run. When using PROC STP, you can send data and parameters to a SAS Stored Process and return data or report results immediately. In this chapter, you will learn how to modify existing stored processes to work with PROC STP, how to send data and prompts to the stored process, and retrieve data from the stored process.

12.1 Understanding STP Procedure Syntax

The following code shows the STP Procedure syntax. The STP procedure contains separate statements for input and output control. You can use datasets or files, and you are not constrained to use the STP parameters only once. For example, listing multiple OUTPUTDATA statements allows you to retrieve multiple datasets. Simply separate the additional statements with semicolons.

```
PROC STP PROGRAM=metadata-path-of-stored-process
               <ODSOUT=STORE | REPLAY>;
  INPUTDATA stored-process-data-file=member-name | 'data-set-path';
  INPUTFILE stored-process-file<=local-fileref | 'local-file-path'>┬;
  INPUTPARAM parameter-name<='parameter-value'> <parameter-name<'parameter-value'>;

  LIST< GROUP=level | (level1...leveln)>;

  LOG FILE=local-fileref | local-file-path

  OUTPUTDATA stored-process-data-file=member-name | 'data-set-path=;
  OUTPUTFILE stored-process-file<=local-fileref |'local-file-path'>;
  OUTPUTPARAM parameter-name<=local-variable-name>;
RUN;
```

12.2 Execution Environment

When a stored process runs from the SAS Stored Process Web Application, the SAS Object Spawner pre-assigns the metadata library, which makes the data available. However, when running this code from PROC STP, the options, libraries, catalogs, and macros that are automatically available to the SAS Stored Process and SAS Workspace Servers do not exist. This is because the stored process is now running in a separate, disconnected SAS session. To push this type of information from the local SAS session to the stored process code, we recommend including the paths as parameters from the INPUTPARM option or setting options within the stored process code itself in order to locate the required objects.

Note: The PROC STP results return a transient package to the user's window.

PROC STP executes the .sas file from the application and machine running the PROC therefore certain scenarios are better suited for running PROC STP than others.

- Run the stored process in a batch step on the SAS Server overnight

- Execute one stored process from another to reduce coding steps

- Request results through SAS Enterprise Guide

#49   **We recommend using SAS Enterprise Guide when executing PROC STP for remote stored process servers.**

When running PROC STP from a local BASE SAS session, the stored process code must reside within the metadata rather than as a separate .sas file in order for the local BASE SAS session to find and execute the code successfully. More information on storing the stored process code in metadata is found in Section 1.2.4, "Using the Source Code".

12.3 Library Definitions

If any resources require metadata authentication and access, the STP procedure works only when you define the metadata access within the stored process. For example, if the stored process was missing the library definition in Example 10-1, users would see an error message similar to the following. This error message indicates that the library was not available along with additional error messages.

```
ERROR: Libname BOOKSAMP is not assigned.
WARNING: No data sets qualify for WHERE processing.
ERROR: No data set open to look up variables.
```

Thus, it is best practice to include a META LIBNAME statement within your stored process code. This method takes information from the user or automatically from the user's connection and assigns the library to the session. See Section 1.3.3, "Accessing Data Libraries" for more information about working with meta libraries.

#50   **We believe that it is ALWAYS a best practice to include the meta library definition in any stored process.**

12.4 First STP Procedure Example

In this example, you want to see the report generated by the stored process "Create Sample" that was shown in Figure 1-3. When running from SAS Enterprise Guide, the results are returned to the local Output window.

Example 12-A STP Sample	Notes
```options metaserver="server" metaport=8561 metauser="user" metapass="pwd";```	Insert the server, user, port, and password to establish a connection to the SAS Metadata Server. This section is not required if you are running the proc stp code below from Enterprise Guide connected to and running the code on the SAS server.
```proc stp program="/Projects/STP Book/Create Sample"```	List the name of the stored process and its location in the metadata. You must use the exact path and name.
``` odsout=replay; run;```	Send the ODS result to the Output window.

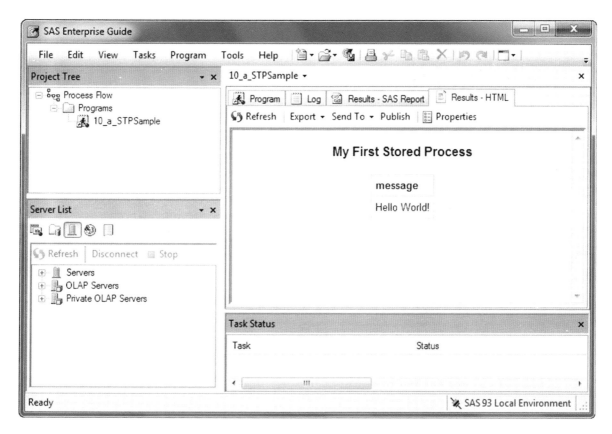

Figure 12-1 Sample PROC STP result from a SAS Enterprise Guide session

12.5 Retrieving Results

You can use data created by stored process to send data to a stored process for evaluation.

12.5.1 Extracting Data Tables using OUTPUTDATA

In Section 8.1.1, "Creating Data Sources for Users" we created data from two different sources so that the results would be available to the SAS BI Dashboard. In this example, the Candy Company analyst would like to use that data for additional analysis.

Use the OUTPUTDATA statement to indicate which dataset you want returned to your local session. Before creating your PROC STP code, you must change the stored process you are going to run from PROC STP so that it responds appropriately.

Therefore, edit the stored process Example 8-A BID Data Source that was created in Section 8.1.1. One of the main changes required to the prior example is that instead of using direct table references, such as WORK.RECENTUNIT, we need to point to metadata parameters to define the tables, such as using &_TARGET_**outdata**.

Note: The **OUTDATA** statement corresponds to the **Table Parameter Name** in the PROC STP step.

Included below are the modifications made to Example 8-A *BID Data Source*.

Before	After

```data recentunit;```
```set result1 result2;```
```run;```
	```data &_TARGET_outdata;```
	```set result1 result2;```
	```run;```

***	***

```call insert_dataset(pid, "WORK", "recentunit",```
```"Last 3 month unit sales sold",```
``` '', rc);```
	```call insert_dataset(pid, "WORK",```
	```"&_TARGET_outdata",```
	``` "Last 3 month unit sales sold", '',```
	```rc);```

The PROC STP OUTPUTDATA statement can now use outdata=*localname* to retrieve the result.

In Section 8.1.1, we only selected the Package Result capability, return to the **Execution** tab in the Metadata Registration and select **Stream** as well.

Hint: To ensure that Example 8-A BID Data Source continues to run from other components, follow the steps in Section 12.6, "Update Metadata Registration".

The analyst would use the following PROC STP code from their local SAS Enterprise Guide session to retrieve the RECENTUNIT data set.

Example 12-C STP Data Retrieval	Notes

```options```
```metaserver="server" metaport=8561```
```metauser="user" metapass="pwd";```
	Insert the server, user, port, and password to establish a connection to the SAS Metadata Server.

```proc stp```
```program="/Projects/STP```
```Book/12_b_biddatasourceedits";```
	Point to the metadata path and stored process name. This must appear exactly as shown in the metadata.

```inputparam region="West";```	The INPUTPARAM statement assigns the Region prompt with the "West" value. This is equivalent to the statement:

Example 12-C STP Data Retrieval	Notes
	%let region=West;
| ```
outputdata
    outdata=work.recentunit;
run;
``` | Use the OUTPUTDATA statement to request the &_TARGET_outdata and return as work.recentunit. |
| ```
title1 'Result';
proc print data=work.recentunit;
run;
``` | Print the resulting dataset for verification. |

12.6 Updating the Metadata Registration

It is good practice to update the stored process metadata registration with these changes described in this section. This provides additional information to the developer that is searchable from the Web application. Follow these steps to modify the stored process metadata registration so that it includes the &_TARGET table information.

1. From the SAS Management Console, edit the stored process. From the **Data** tab, in the Targets area, create a new &_TARGET_ value.

2. In the **Table parameter name** field, type **outdata**. Use the same name used in the code from Section 12.5.1, "Extracting Data Tables using OUTPUTDATA".

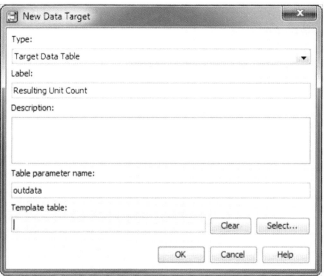

12.6.1 Reports using OUTPUTFILE Parameter

You can also send data to, as well as receive reports from, stored processes. The analyst from the Candy Company has asked for the ability to send any SAS dataset into the Pareto stored process created in Section 7.3.2, "Using Data Sources and Targets". This will enable use by Microsoft Excel users. The stored process was written to accept remote data source targets; therefore, the PROC STP is the only information that is required by the analyst.

1. Because the input file is in a different format for the PROC STP than the SAS Add-in to Microsoft Office, we should (but are not required to) update the stored process metadata registration to include both options. From the Data tab, select **New for Sources** and enter a second possible source stream for NEWDAT2.

   If the Generic Data Source option appears rather than Generic Stream, your stored process is not compatible with SAS Add-in to MS Office 4.3.

2. Update the SAS program code to accommodate both scenarios - one for the Add-in Input Stream and one for the PROC STP input.

Example 12-D Pareto for AMO and Data table	Notes
`%stpbegin;`	
`%global dat;`	Add a global statement for DAT. This allows this macro to be used elsewhere in the system

`%macro loc;`
`%if`
`%substr(%quote(&_CLIENT), 1, 7)`
`=PROCSTP %then %do;`
`  goptions device=java;`
`  %let dat=&_SOURCE_NEWDAT2;`
`%end;`
`%else %do;`
`libname newdat xml;`
`%let dat=newdat.&_WEBIN_SASNAME;`
`%end;`
`%mend;`
`%loc;`
	Use the _CLIENT reserved macro variable to assign the **&dat** variable to either the XML input stream (for Add-in Input) or to the PROC STP input stream.

Example 12-D Pareto for AMO and Data table	Notes

``
proc freq data=&dat noprint;
tables &var1 / out=temp norow
nocol;
weight &var2;
run;
``
	Use the **&dat** new macro variable to run the remaining steps.

``
proc sort data=work.temp;
by descending percent;
run;
data temp2(drop=newcount);
set temp end=last;
total+percent;
if total <=80 then output;
if total > 80 then do;
  &var1='Other';
  newcount+count;
end;
if last then do;
  count=newcount;
  output;
end;
run;
``
	The remaining steps are the same.

``
proc sql noprint;
 select &var1 into :vals separated by '"   "'
from work.temp2;
 quit;
axis1 order=("&vals");
``	

``
proc gchart data=work.temp2;
 vbar &var1/sumvar=count maxis=axis1;
run; quit;
%stpbegin;
``	

When accessing the new stored process from Add-in to MS Office, you will notice that both the Excel and SAS Dataset prompts appear. Users will need to enter a valid cell value or range in the SAS Dataset prompt, however only the Excel range is used.

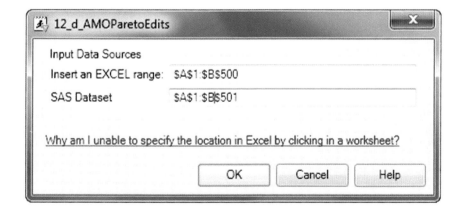

3. Use PROC STP to access the Pareto report.

Example 12-E Sending Data Into Pareto STP	Notes
```options metaserver="server" metaport=8561 metauser="user" metapass="pwd"; ```	Insert the server, user, port, and password to establish a connection to the SAS Metadata Server.
```goptions device=actximg;```	Specify any graphical options to be applied to the results.
```proc stp program="/Projects/STP Book/12_d_amoParetoEdits"; ```	
```inputdata newdat2=sashelp.shoes;```	Use INPUTDATA to provide the ability to push data into the stored process. Newdat2 corresponds directly to the defined fileref in Step 1 above
```inputparam var1='region'; inputparam var2='sales'; ```	Provide the values for the other parameters in the stored process.
```outputfile _webout="c:\temp\pareto.html"; run; ```	Point the _webout location to a local file folder so that the results are retrievable.

12.6.2 Reports using ODSOUT

In the prior example, the report was written to a permanent location - c:\temp\pareto.html. To write the report to a temporary path, you can use the ODSOUT option as shown in the following example.

Example 12-F Temporary Output Destination	Notes
```options metaserver="server" metaport=8561 metauser="user" metapass="pwd"; goptions device=actximg; proc stp program="/Projects/STP Book/12_d_amoParetoEdits" ```	
```ODSOUT=REPLAY```	Odsout=replay writes the results into the SAS Enterprise Guide session's temporary work output and displays immediately to the user.
```; inputdata newdat2=sashelp.shoes; inputparam var1='region'; inputparam var2='sales'; outputfile _webout="c:\temp\pareto.html"; run; ```	Note that the ODSOUT option resides within the PROC STP statement; therefore, the semicolon closes the statement.

The results are viewable immediately within your SAS Enterprise Guide project.

12.7 Sending Values into Prompts

The greatest value from stored processes is the ability to send different values to the prompt for the answers. In this example, you will learn how to send values to the prompts.

12.7.1 Working with Date Ranges

You can set stored process date input parameters in the format DDMONYYYY and surround the parameter with quotes. Unlike SAS code, do not add a "d" suffix to the date. In the following example, note that the automatic macro variables, such as SALE_DATE_MIN and SALE_DATE_MAX, are not needed. SAS takes the SALE_DATE multiple values, converts to the range (_MIN and _MAX) variables, and automatically creates the associated variables (such as _LABEL).

Example 12-G Sending Date Prompt Values	Notes

```options```
 ```metaserver="server"```
 ```metaport=8561```
 ```metauser="user"```
 ```metapass="pwd";```
	Insert the server, user, port, and password to establish a connection to the SAS Metadata Server.

```proc stp program="/Projects/STP``` ```Book/02_c_multiselect" odsout=replay;```	Request that the stored process results are returned to the user session immediately.
```inputparam prodprompt="BED"```	
```SALE_DATE="01NOV2010"``` ```SALE_DATE="01NOV2011";```	Submit the first and last date values that make up the **SALE_DATE** range.
```run;```	

The range values must be in the order expected (smaller values before larger values). Otherwise, when you have alternated between the two SALE_DATE INPUTPARAMS your code generates an error message similar to the following:

```
NOTE: PROC_STP: ====== Proc STP Execution Starting ======
NOTE: PROC_STP: ====== Stored Process:  /Projects/STP Book/02_c_multiselect ======
ERROR: STP: An error occurred preprocessing input parameters:
com.sas.prompts.InvalidPromptValueException: An error occurred for the prompt "Select a date
range:" (values: November 01, 2011 -- November 01, 2010).The lower boundary for
the value is greater than the upper boundary of the value: November 01, 2011 -- November 01, 2010
.

NOTE: PROC_STP: ====== Stored Process: /Projects/STP Book/02_c_multiselect  Return Status =
      1012 ======
NOTE: PROC_STP: ====== Proc STP Execution Ending ======
NOTE: The SAS System stopped processing this step because of errors.
NOTE: PROCEDURE STP used (Total process time):
      real time           8.92 seconds
      cpu time            0.04 seconds
```

12.7.2 Using Multiple Selection Prompts

To use PROC STP with more than one prompt value, use the same prompt name multiple times. Doing this allows SAS to convert the proper macro values suffixed with the count automatically.

Example 12-H Sending Multiple Prompt Values	Notes

`options`
`metaserver="server"`
`metaport=8561`
`metauser="user"`
`metapass="pwd";`	

`proc stp program="/Projects/STP`
`Book/02_c_multiselect" odsout=replay;`
`inputparam`	

`    prodprompt="BED"`
`    prodprompt="CHAIR"`
`    prodprompt="SOFA"`
	Multiple values are submitted to the Multiple Selection stored process.

`SALE_DATE="01NOV2010"`
`SALE_DATE="01NOV2011";`
`run;`	

Index

A

action, 55
  background, 57, 108
  data, 58
  newwindow, 58
  nobanner, 56, 58
  notimer, 56
  program, 56
  properties, 56
  tree, 55
  XML, 4
ActiveX Image, 48
Add-in for Microsoft Office, 1, 89
  Excel as data source, 90
  Pareto chart, 90
  running a stored process, 89
  SAS Central, 90
Allow execution on other applications servers, 8
Allow execution on selected application server only, 8
appearance
  graphics output, 46
  layout, 49
  style sheet, 42
application server, 7
attachment
  coding, 133
AUTOEXEC.SAS, 13
automatic variable name, 25

B

batch process
  PROC STP, 4
  SAS 9.2 and prior, 4
BI Dashboard, 1, 95
  custom indicators, 103
  data sources, 95

C

CARD/CARD4 statement
  advantages, 121
  coding, 121, 125
  variables, 122
CARD/CARDS4 statement, 142
chaining reports, 35
coding
  add fields, 132

appearance, 41
append data set from input data, 135
changes for stored process, 18
convert existing code, 15
date prompts, 19
email message, 148
error trapping, 116
first stored process, 15
HTML forms, 120, 124, 130
JavaScript, 138
layout, 49
linking graphs, 53
linking reports, 35
logic test, 133
logs, 60
message to user, 116
multiple selections, 23
optional prompts, 27
output format, 144
prompt groups, 30
prompts, 18
quoting, 18
quoting, 122
upload file, 133
comma-separated values (CSV), 130
compatible, 63
configuration files, 60
custom form, 125

D

data libraries, 13
data sources, 10, 70, 88, 95, 158
data table
  storage, 12
data tables. *See also* library
data targets, 10, 70, 90, 158
datalines. *See* CARD/CARD4 statement
date range, 19
dates
  prompts, 19
  range, 19
  working with, 21
device drivers, 47
display as hyperlink check box, 88

E

edit source code button, 11
email messages, 151

mobile devices, 150

N

no_bottom_matter option, 139
no_top_matter option, 139

O

ODS HTML statement, 139, *See also* HTML coding
   changes for stored process, 18
   coding options, 139
   no_bottom_matter, 139
   no_top_matter, 139
   usage, 125
   using with stored process, 138
ODS LAYOUT statement
   coding, 52
   example, 51
ODS REGION
   statement, 52
options
   fullstimer, 61
   mlogic, 60
   mprint, 60
   nomlogic, 60
   nomprint, 60
output
   ActiveX charts, 46
   email, 148
   HTML, 11, 46, 47, 144
   Java charts, 46
   PDF, 46, 144, 149, 150
   RTF, 47, 144
   XML, 11

P

package result, 97, 105
   _debug_file parameter, 60
   background processing, 109
   BI Dashboard, 96
   channel, 11
   defined, 11
   email, 11
   permanent, 11
   portlet, 110
   SAS Publishing Framework, 97
   stored process reports, 4, 111
   transient, 11
   Web Report Studio, 82
   WebDAV, 11
parameters tab
   add group prompt, 31
   adding prompts, 17
   dependent prompts, 33
   editing prompts, 24
   editing shared prompts, 146

multiple prompts, 20
   registeration, 9
   shared prompts, 42, 146
Pareto chart, 90
pdf, 150
PDF, 130
PNG, 47
PRINT procedure
   used in stored process, 19
PROC procedure
   used in stored process, 26
PROC STP, 78
   coding, 155
   data tables, 156
   debugging, 153
   INPUTDATA statement, 160
   INPUTPARAM statement, 161
   metadata access, 153
   metadata registration, 157
   ODSOUT statement, 160
   OUTPUTDATA statement, 156
   OUTPUTFILE parameter, 158
   prompts, 161, 162
   prompts example, 162
   syntax, 153
ProcessBody comment, 4
prompt
   cascading group, 79
   on webpage, 138
prompts
   _debug, 46
   _gopt_device, 46
   _odsdest, 46
   _properties, 58
   Add-In for MS Office, 91
   adding, 9, 69
   allow multiple selections, 25
   coding, 18, 22, 25, 26, 29, 34, 74, 116, 118, 156, 160
   creating a prompt, 9
   date, 19
   date range, 19, 22, 161
   default values, 56
   dependent, 33
   displayed value, 33
   editing, 9
   email, 148
   errors, 116
   formatted value, 33
   graphs, 30
   groups, 9, 30
     removing, 49
   hidden, 59, 74, 108
   information map, 73, 79
   inputparam, 156, 160, 161
     errors, 161
   invalid, 116
   multiple selections, 23, 26, 27, 162
   new, 9

Made in the USA
Lexington, KY
12 April 2013